OEDIPUS AND AKHNATON

Books by Immanuel Velikovsky

WORLDS IN COLLISION (1950)

AGES IN CHAOS: *From Exodus to King Akhnaton* (1952)

EARTH IN UPHEAVAL (1955)

OEDIPUS AND AKHNATON (1960)

OEDIPUS AND AKHNATON

Myth and History

IMMANUEL VELIKOVSKY

Garden City, New York

DOUBLEDAY & COMPANY, INC.

1960

Quotation on page 196 from The Basic Writings of Sigmund Freud, *trans. and ed. by Dr. A. A. Brill. Copyright 1938 by Random House, Inc. Reprinted by permission of the Brill Trust.*

Quotations from The Complete Greek Drama, *ed. by Whitney J. Oates and Eugene O'Neill, Jr., by permission of Random House, Inc.*

To Horace M. Kallen

Contents

CONTENTS

PART II

Illustrations

ILLUSTRATIONS

ILLUSTRATIONS

Foreword

Two decades ago, on the shore of the eastern Mediterranean, somewhere between Egypt and Greece, I read Freud's last book, *Moses and Monotheism,* and was prompted to read more about Akhnaton, the real hero of that book. Soon I was struck by some close parallels between this Egyptian king and the legendary Oedipus. A few months later I found myself in the libraries of the New World, among many large volumes containing the records of excavations in Thebes and el-Amarna. This study carried me into the larger field of Egyptian history and to the concept of *Ages in Chaos*—a reconstruction of twelve hundred years of ancient history, twelve years of toil. My work on Oedipus and Akhnaton, in the form of many notes and a short draft, rested all that time and more; Horace's advice to withhold a manuscript from publication for nine years was complied with—doubly so. More than eighteen years passed from the conception of the work and its first draft to its rewriting and preparation for the printer.

The delay was of great benefit to the work. In the intervening years several important papers on Pharaoh Akhnaton and his house were published; these disclosed archaeological facts from which I could draw added support for my theory.

History threw light on the old legend; but the old legend also threw light on history. "The reign of Akhnaton, for seventeen years Pharaoh of Egypt, stands out as the most interesting epoch in the long sequence of Egyptian history," wrote Arthur Weigall, adding, "there is probably no period in ancient history which so merits elucidation."[1] This much is known: the religious reform of Akhnaton was abolished, his line died out, and his palaces and city were abandoned; history, however, professes not to know the cause of all this, nor the personal fate of Akhnaton, nor what happened during the anarchy which followed or perhaps preceded the end of this glorious dynasty. But the end of Akhnaton, the fate of his two youthful successors, Smenkhkare and Tutankhamen, the decay of the kingdom, and the fate of Thebes—all are understood with the help of a cycle of legends that persisted in the eastern Mediterranean and on Greek soil. The mysterious relationships, the incomprehensible finds in the graves, the enigmatic sequence of events, once illuminated by the legend, are no longer obscure and secret. The light of the legend carried away, the historical facts and finds glow with their own light, and the inner relationships are understood on the strength of these facts and finds themselves.

Oedipus and Akhnaton can be read entirely independently of any other work of mine. Yet it properly follows *Ages in Chaos*, Volume I, which covered the time from the great upheaval that closed the Middle Kingdom in Egypt to the time of Pharaoh Akhnaton. The present short book tells his story and that of the tragic events at the end of the Eighteenth Dynasty. In its wake, another volume of *Ages in Chaos*, too long postponed, will be concluded, bringing my historical reconstruction to the advent of Alexander.

It is an ironic connotation of this work that both Oedipus and Akhnaton were Freud's heroes. He did not realize their close resemblance, even identity; he saw in one the symbolic

[1] *The Life and Times of Akhnaton* (1922), Preface.

figure of a sinner, tortured by the sinful but all too human urges to which he submits, and in the other a saint, "the first monotheist," and precursor of Moses, the lawgiver. Unavoidably, the story touches on an important point in the history of religion. The road to monotheism was thorny and tortuous. Akhnaton, however, was not "the first monotheist"; that he was called "the criminal" by later pharaohs was not so much the result of his attempts at religious reform as of something else, the story of which forms the content of these pages.

IMMANUEL VELIKOVSKY

January, 1960

ACKNOWLEDGMENTS

During the work of final preparation of the manuscript (September 1958–November 1959), Dr. Walter Federn, Egyptologist and bibliographer, was of singular help to me as a source of information and as a guide through the vast Egyptological literature. The script that I regarded as close to final was enriched by several important pieces of evidence from the store of Egyptian archaeological material and from the incessant debate in periodicals encompassing a series of unresolved problems in the field. Dr. Federn's assistance was given in a generous spirit of constructive criticism, regardless of whether or not he agreed with me on any point. The basic idea and the plan of the book, its details, and its conclusions being mine, I assume sole responsibility for them.

Mrs. Kathryn Tebbel and Miss Marion Kuhn read the manuscript with great care and smoothed many a rough spot in my exposition. Elliott Schryver, a senior editor, and the rest of the staff at Doubleday gave me the kind of assistance that an author prays for.

PART I

The Legend

THE Greek legend of the patricide who married his mother and sired children in incest is over twenty-seven centuries old. For a few hundred years it was carried by word of mouth and was recited as a poem of which only a few lines survive; then, in the form of plays written by Aeschylus, Sophocles, and Euripides, followed by many lesser authors, it gained a conspicuous place in the literature of the classical period, of the Middle Ages, and of modern times as well. The story seized the human imagination, and its grip has not weakened even after almost three millennia.

Sigmund Freud explained the Oedipus legend as having grown out of the unconscious desire of a son to possess his mother and to dispose of his father by murder. From the folklore of primitive peoples Sir James Frazer gathered together many instances that Freud used to substantiate his theory: in the Stone Age the grown-up sons of the cave man, the undisputed despot in the cave, usually murdered him in order to possess his wives, their mothers. In the neurotic make-up of modern man the Oedipus complex, according to the psychoanalytical theory, plays a prominent role; in the opinion of the analysts the behavior of neurotics and the content of their dreams, as recorded in innumerable medical case histories, support Freud's theory.

The subconscious urge to possess the mother, as concealed

in or revealed by dreams, was not unknown to the ancients. Sophocles, in his *Oedipus Rex*, had Jocasta, still unaware that Oedipus was her son, say to him: "Fear not that marriage with thy mother; such things men oft have dreams of; but who cares least about them lives the happiest."[1]

The early rabbis, authors of the Talmud, knew how, through skillful interpretation, to bring to light the "Oedipus complex." In the chapter on dream interpretation in the Tractate Brakhot of the Babylonian Talmud, it is said in the name of Rabbi Ishmael that if one dreams that he pours oil on an olive tree he is possessed by the desire for incestuous relations with his mother.[2]

Is the Oedipus legend, then, a myth, a poetic creation that sprang from the subconscious mind, based on no actual and specific historical happening? Was there no historical King Oedipus and no Jocasta, his mother, whom he wedded, and no Laius, his father, whom he killed? Or is the Oedipus legend based on a historical occurrence? If the latter is true, its hold on the imagination of the literati through the ages could be explained as a real experience that has been echoed in the dark recesses of many human souls.

This question of the historicity of the Oedipus story has long occupied the minds of classical scholars, but no lead has ever been found. Though a multitude of poets[3] and more than a

[1] In *The Complete Greek Drama*, trans. R. C. Jebb, ed. Whitney J. Oates and Eugene O'Neill, Jr. (1938). The subject is discussed in Plato, *Republic*, Book IX. Julius Caesar on the night before he crossed the Rubicon had an incestuous dream about his mother, which was interpreted as an augury of victory and conquest. Suetonius, *Julius Caesar*, 7; Plutarch, *Lives*, Caesar, 32.

[2] See my article, "Psychoanalytische Ahnungen in der Traumdeutungskunst der alten Hebräer nach dem Traktat Brachot," *Psychoanalytische Bewegung*, V (1933), published by Internationaler Psychoanalytischer Verlag, Vienna.

[3] Among the early poets, Homer, Hesiod, and Pindar alluded to the Theban tragedy. Antimachus of Teos wrote a Thebaid; so also did Antagoras of Rhodes, Menelaus of Aegae, and Nicander of Colophon.

few historians of Greece and Rome referred to Oedipus and his tragic fate,[4] they obviously alluded to the story elaborated by the great poets, Aeschylus, Sophocles, and Euripides.

In post-classical times, in the second century of the present era, at various locations near Thebes and Colonus in Greece, tombs were pointed out to a traveling historian, Pausanias, as the sepulchers of the heroes of the Oedipus cycle. However, "three of the tombs and cult places ascribed to Oedipus are certainly late,"[5] only the tomb of Eteonus in Boeotia can claim antiquity, and there is nothing to show that it bears any relation to Oedipus. "Where he was buried, none knew in later times."[6]

Nothing that has been found in the excavations in Greece and the Helladic islands testifies to the historicity of King Oedipus and the royal house of Laius in general.

"I am persuaded that the origin of Oedipus is to be found not in history but in folk-tales," wrote one authority; it dates back to Mycenaean times, yet it was only a folk tale.[7] But not every scholar subscribes to the mythological character of the story. H. J. Rose says in *Modern Methods in Classical Mythology*, "If some day a clearly identifiable relic of the veritable Oidipus were to reward an excavator, as Priam's city [Troy] did the faith of Schliemann, I would be gratified, but not in the least surprised."[8]

The earliest reference to the Oedipus legend is found in Homer's *Odyssey*. The epic was most probably put into writing early in the seventh century before the present era; it describes the travels and wanderings of Odysseus after the fall of Troy,

---

[4] Among them Pherecydes, Hellanicos, Diodorus, Nicolas of Damascus, Apollodorus, Hyginus, Palaiphatos, Malalas, John of Antioch.

[5] M. P. Nilsson, *The Mycenaean Origin of Greek Mythology* (California University Press, 1932), p. 103.

[6] H. J. Rose, *Modern Methods in Classical Mythology* (1930), p. 27.

[7] Nilsson, *The Mycenaean Origin of Greek Mythology*, p. 103.

[8] Rose, *Modern Methods in Classical Mythology*, p. 28.

in the siege of which he had participated. The wanderer also visited Hades, the abode of the departed. There he saw the unfortunate mother-wife of Oedipus; Homer called her Epicaste:

"And I saw the mother of Oedipodes, fair Epicaste, who wrought a monstrous deed in ignorance of mind in that she wedded her own son, and he, when he had slain his own father, wedded her, and straightway the gods made these things known among men. . . . She made fast a noose on high from a lofty beam, overpowered by her sorrow."[9]

It is generally accepted that the Oedipus cycle of legends is of greater antiquity than the so-called Homeric cycle of the siege of Troy by the Greeks or Achaeans under Agamemnon, and older, too, than the time of the Tyrants, Thyestes and his brother Atreus, father of Agamemnon. The inclusion of a short reference to the Oedipus tragedy in the *Odyssey* permits us to deduce only that the legend is older than the seventh century, the time when the Homeric epics were put into writing. However, in finding the time of the origin of the legend one does not solve the problem of whether or not the origin had its roots in historical happenings. To enable us to deal with this question in more detail, let us relate the legend as it is known from Greek tragedians and other writers.

The Theban King Laius and his wife Jocasta were long childless. Eventually she conceived, but the oracle prophesied that the son to be born would kill his father and marry his mother. When the child was born he was given to a royal servant to be carried away to a wasteland and abandoned there to die with his feet pierced through. But the child was given to or was found by a shepherd and was cared for by him and his wife. Later they took the child to Corinth to the royal palace of Polybus and Merope, who adopted him and called him Oedipus because of his swollen feet. There he grew up thinking himself

[9] Homer, *The Odyssey*, trans. A. T. Murray (Loeb Classical Library), XI, 271ff.

to be the true son of the royal couple. A remark by one of the guests at a banquet in the palace made the youth wonder about his origin, and he traveled to the oracle at Delphi, where he heard that he was doomed to be a patricide. Horrified, he failed to return to the palace of Polybus to avoid his predestined fate.

Wandering in desolate regions, he met, near a place where three roads ran together, his real father, King Laius, traveling in a chariot. The driver of the chariot struck the youth, who was slow to yield the way, with his whip, and the youth killed the driver and his master. Continuing on his way unconcerned, he came to Thebes. The approach to the city was guarded by the Sphinx, a winged maiden-monster. Everyone who tried to enter the city was stopped by the Sphinx, who put a riddle to the new arrival; if the riddle was not solved, as was regularly the case, the stranger met death at the hands of the maiden-monster.

The Sphinx posed this question to Oedipus: Who is it that walks in the morning on four, on two during the day, and on three in the evening? Oedipus solved the riddle: it is man. In infancy he crawls on four, as a man he walks on two, in old age he moves about leaning on a cane.

Upon hearing the correct answer, the Sphinx in chagrin killed herself by leaping from the rock. Oedipus entered Thebes, and the citizens, thankful to him for having delivered the city from the monster, offered the newcomer their queen, recently widowed, to be his wife, together with the kingdom.

Oedipus lived happily with Jocasta, not knowing that she was his mother; she bore him children, two sons, Polynices and Eteocles, and two daughters, Antigone and Ismene. He was respected and loved by his subjects and was looked on as a just and wise man.

Then came a sign from heaven—a plague or a famine or some other distress. When the oracle was queried as to what had caused the displeasure of the gods, the answer was that in their midst a crime had been committed: a son had killed his father and continued to live unpunished among them. To propitiate the gods, the criminal must be killed or driven into exile. In ever growing tension, out of the questioning of various witnesses—the servant who carried the baby to the wasteland and the shepherd who saved him—the truth slowly dawned on Oedipus. Jocasta hanged herself in despair; in his anguish Oedipus blinded himself and soon thereafter left the throne and the city, an exile.

In all these doings an important role fell to Creon, the brother of Jocasta. He grew inimical to Oedipus and insisted on his punishment.

One of Oedipus' daughters, Antigone, accompanied her blind and homeless father on his wanderings. In Thebes the elder son, Polynices, occupied the throne on the condition that he would vacate it after a year in favor of the younger Eteocles and reoccupy it after another year, the two brothers thus reigning in turn. Creon was instrumental in bringing about this arrangement. But when the time came for Eteocles to return the throne to Polynices he refused to do so, supported in his refusal by Creon, the true ruler of the land.

With a confederate army of foreigners assembled for him by his father-in-law Adrastus, king of Argos, Polynices besieged Thebes. At the seven gates of the seven-gated Thebes seven leaders from each side met in two-man combat; Polynices and Eteocles opposed each other, and each killed the other, thus fulfilling the curse of their father Oedipus, who was bitter at having been expelled from the city by his sons.

Creon forbade the burial of Polynices because he had warred against his city and people, and he proclaimed that whoever dared to disobey his order would die; the body of Polynices must be left where he fell for the birds and dogs to devour. For Eteocles, however, he ordered national mourning and many rites and a splendid tomb furnished with mortuary gifts, and he himself, now king of the realm, presided over the funeral rites.

Antigone could not suffer her brother to remain unburied, and she disobeyed Creon's decree. When she was apprehended she was condemned by Creon to die a slow death immured in a cave-tomb.

When another generation grew up the sons of the seven fallen heroes came once more to renew the siege of Thebes, and these scions, known as Epigoni, succeeded where their fathers had failed, and took the city.

The house of Laius was doomed, and no effort to change its predestined fate availed at all. The legend has it also that this · doom was visited on Laius and his house because he was the first to introduce unnatural love on the soil of Greece: he corrupted a youth, Chrysippus.

The story as told here follows in the main Sophocles' version as given by him in his trilogy, *Oedipus Rex*, *Oedipus at Colonus*, and *Antigone*. Among the versions of Sophocles, Euripides, and Aeschylus there are many differences. Aeschylus, too, wrote a trilogy, of which only *The Seven against Thebes* remains; *Laius* and *Oedipus* are not extant. Euripides likewise wrote several plays on the cycle, of which *The Phoenissae* remains.[10] Differing from Sophocles, Aeschylus and Euripides made Eteocles the elder brother, and while Euripides took the side of Polynices, Aeschylus sided with Eteocles.

However, in the legend as it is known from other sources there are greater variances. According to one version, Oedipus killed Laius, not at a chance meeting, but defending or avenging Chrysippus. A version current in antiquity had it that Oedipus' children were borne, not by his mother-wife, Jocasta, but by another wife of his, Euryganeia; in another version,

---

[10] Besides this, in *The Suppliants* Euripides deals with an event closely related to the Theban drama.

some of the children were by Jocasta and others by Euryganeia; in still another, he had a third marriage with a virgin, Astymedusa.[11] Also, in some variants Oedipus did not go into exile but continued to live in a palace in Thebes, as a prisoner; or he was exiled, though not immediately after leaving the throne, by Polynices, who ruled first. This last point is found also in Sophocles' version, in *Oedipus at Colonus* ("Villain, who when thou hadst the sceptre and the throne, which now thy brother hath in Thebes, dravest me, thine own father, into exile, and madest me citiless . . ."). Euripides had Jocasta live till the fraternal duel between Polynices and Eteocles and try in vain to forestall it. Many other variations are found among the poets and tragedians.

According to the legendary chronology, the war of the Seven against Thebes took place twenty years before the beginning of the war against Troy and thirty years before the capture of that fortress; the war of the Epigoni against Thebes was placed ten or fourteen years after the Seven against Thebes and thus only a few years before the start of the expedition under Agamemnon. Several scholars[12] took "this myth to be a historical reminiscence of a war waged against Thebes by a confederation of Argive princes."[13] But the very historicity of the Trojan War was questioned, and heroes of the ancient legends of the Homeric and Theban cycles were even more often characterized as mythological personages.

More skeptical than others as to the historicity of legendary figures in general, and especially so concerning the traditions of the races that did not achieve literacy, is Lord Raglan. In his book *The Hero*[14] he quotes another author: "The folk have

[11] E. Bethe, *Thebanische Heldenlieder* (1891), pp. 23, 26.

[12] Wilamowitz, E. Meyer, C. Robert.

[13] Nilsson, *The Mycenaean Origin of Greek Mythology*, p. 107.

[14] Oxford University Press, 1937.

no sense of history; there would be nothing improbable to them in St. George meeting Napoleon in the same ballad." Not only are places and events distorted and displaced in "race memory" or folk tradition, but they are in the majority of cases straight inventions. "The rapidity with which historical events are forgotten shows how unlikely it is that what is remembered in the form of tradition should be history." More often than not traditions tell the stories of kings and queens and the royal household. "Now the stories of court life that get abroad today are always inaccurate and often quite untrue, and we have no reason to believe that things were different a thousand or five thousand years ago."

According to Lord Raglan, something approaching the historical truth can be claimed only in those cases where we have contemporary written statements of participants or witnesses; ancient sagas, transmitted in the majority of cases by illiterate people, cannot be said to contain material for history. "Such terms as 'race-memory' or 'folk-memory' suggest that there exists in every illiterate community something analogous to our Public Record Office, and obscure the fact that every unwritten tradition must be transmitted by conscious individual effort at least once in each generation."[15]

The legendary heroes are, in Raglan's opinion, but inventions which conform to a pattern. This pattern combines the following features:

"The hero's mother is a royal virgin; his father is a king, and often a near relative of his mother, but the circumstances of his conception are unusual, and he is also reputed to be the son of a god. At birth an attempt is made, usually by his father or his maternal grandfather [or the overlord of the realm], to kill him, but he is spirited away, and reared by foster-parents in a far country. We are told nothing of his childhood, but on reaching manhood he returns or goes to his future kingdom.

[15] Ibid., pp. 13–17.

27

After a victory over the king and/or a giant, dragon, or wild beast, he marries a princess, often the daughter of his predecessor, and becomes king. For a time he reigns uneventfully, and prescribes laws, but later he loses favour with the gods and/or his subjects, and is driven from the throne and city, after which he meets with a mysterious death, often at the top of a hill. His children, if any, do not succeed him. His body is not buried, but nevertheless he has one or more holy sepulchers."[16]

Lord Raglan applied his pattern to various heroes, starting with Oedipus and going on to Theseus, Romulus, Hercules, Perseus, Jason, Asclepius, Dionysus, Apollo, Zeus, Joseph, Moses, Sigurd, Arthur, Robin Hood, and many more, checking them to see at how many points each legend coincides with the pattern. Oedipus stands at the head of the list, showing the greatest conformity to Lord Raglan's pattern. It is Oedipus, then, even more than Dionysus or Apollo, who is a mythological figure, born in the imagination of bards.

Is there in the patricide of Oedipus possibly an echo of the overthrow of Cronus by Zeus? asked an eminent historian, Eduard Meyer. He saw in Oedipus a transfiguration of Hercules, a god whose life is but a symbolic representation of the yearly cycle of nature; Oedipus espouses his own mother, the mother earth. Some students of classical mythology have seen in Jocasta a personification of Hera, the goddess of the earth,[17] others saw in her a moon goddess.[18] Still other students decried such conjectures as examples of the aberration of comparative mythology.

Can we, for instance, subscribe to an explanation of so complex a story as the Theban tragedy, which assumes that this plot is merely a reflection in the mirror of folklore of the daily

[16] Ibid., pp. 179–80.

[17] O. Gruppe, *Griechische Mythologie* (1906), p. 504.

[18] K. Kunst, *Die Frauengestalten im attischen Drama* (1922).

passage of the sun across the sky from dawn to dark? In the nineteenth century, the age preceding the psychoanalytical treatment of folklore, it was the vogue to explain all kinds of material of mythological or legendary character as invariably symbolizing the daily and yearly movement of the sun amid other seasonal changes. Actually one can trace this prevalent solar explanation of myths to the Latin author of the fourth century of the present era, Macrobius. Friedrich August Wolf (1759–1824), a close friend of Goethe, evolved the theory that the legends and myths of classical Greece and Rome had their origin, not in real events, but in the phenomena of nature. This theory found a considerable following and was further developed by Max Mueller, the scholarly author of numerous works on Hindu lore. The solar explanation was by far the predominant one, and the variety of other natural phenomena was ignored. This method was applied to the legend of Oedipus:

"Oedipus murders his father, weds his mother, and dies a blind old man. The solar hero murders the father who begot him, the darkness; he shares his bed with his mother, the sunset glow from whose womb in the morning dawn he did arise; he dies blinded: the sun goes down."[19]

It is true that many myths and legends reflect happenings in nature—not those that are of everyday occurrence but those that disrupt the even flow of the days and years; and to prove this I presented a vast array of folkloric material in *Worlds in Collision*. The Oedipus legend, however, does not belong in this category: the human character of the drama is too obvious; the mental agony in the conflict between "must" and "must not" is too clearly expressed to permit the origin of this tragedy to be ascribed to the work of unchained elements, still less to daily occurrences in the sky and on the earth. Not the elements of nature but the fate of man is the subject and the plot of the tragedy, and it is human—all too human to be an allusion to

[19] Ignaz Goldziher, *Der Mythos bei den Hebräern* (1876), p. 215.

the cosmic drama, as is, for instance, the story of Phaethon, or of Typhon, or of Pallas Athena.

The content of the Thebaid cycle of legends reveals itself as not homogeneous: political events of a state in peace and war apparently are of a different nature from the human tragedy of fate and doom, though the former could easily serve as the stage for the latter. And these elements, political and personal, are again of a different nature from some clearly mythological subjects. Thus it appears that we would be on the wrong path if we were to try to classify the drama according to single elements in it. Yet there must be some reason for the inclusion in one plot of such heterogeneous elements, political, personal, and mythological.

If, on the assumption that the legend contains some historical happenings, an examination is made of the various elements of the legend to determine which by their nature could be historical and which must be regarded as mythical, one would include in the second category the episode with the Sphinx who guarded the road to Thebes, who posed riddles to all travelers wishing to enter the city and killed herself when Oedipus gave the correct answer. This appears clearly mythical.

The Sphinx

A MONSTER besieges a city or a castle, or sits in watch over a captive maiden or a hidden treasure, and devours those who try to penetrate the castle, find the treasure, or free the maiden. A newcomer, often the youngest among his brothers, or one who is thought to be a fool, kills the monster, usually by a sly stratagem, and wins the castle, the kingdom, the maiden, usually a princess, and the treasure too. This is a widespread motif of great antiquity.

A riddle is given to all pretenders to solve; whoever tries and fails pays with his life or freedom. But the young hero solves the riddle by sheer cleverness or by finding out the answer in a not wholly honest way, and receives his reward. This, too, is an ancient legendary motif, repeatedly found in the tales of many peoples.

In the story of the Sphinx that guarded the city of Thebes in Boeotia, both motifs are tied together. The monster, the Sphinx, kills herself when the hero correctly answers the riddle, and the hero, a poor adventurer but a prince by birth, enters the city and obtains the hand of the widowed queen.

In the stereotype version of the motif, the prince, now a king, reigns happily ever after with his queen—and this is the end of the story.[1] The Oedipus legend, however, has no happy ending; the tragedy starts where bliss is expected to begin.

[1] However, cf. Raglan's view, presented above.

31

Students of the Oedipus legend have observed that the story of the monster was not originally part of the legend, that it is an addition, a later interpolation.[2] Some students, however, wished to see in the destruction of the monster an original part of the myth and to regard everything else as an addition or a later elaboration.[3] Whichever is true, it appears indisputable that the incident with the Sphinx is merely mythological.

A psychoanalyst would be inclined to interpret the Sphinx story, the overcoming of a female monster, as the self-deliverance of a son from the tyranny of an overpowering mother. O. Rank explained the Sphinx as the incarnation of the repulsive traits of the mother; Theodor Reik has also pointed to the similar end of Jocasta and the Sphinx—in suicide.[4] The victory over the Sphinx or the overpowering of the mother is a necessary counterpart to the killing of a father by a son, an action real or symbolic. This splitting of the mother's image into hateful and attractive components could also have been the psychological reason for the incongruous addition: a prince who killed a king takes his queen; why should he be burdened with the riddles of a maiden-monster after having performed the heroic deed of removing the king?

But let us not pass by, like a heedless traveler, the monster sitting on the rock. The creature that watched over Thebes in Boeotia was not one of the familiar Greek figures: the giant Pallas, the Minotaur, the centaur, the Gorgon Medusa, a fury, a cyclops. It was the Sphinx, and so it is called by the Greek tragedians. Her land of origin was Egypt;[5] although her images were found in many countries, including Crete and Mycenae in Greece, they were either imports from Egypt or, as is as-

[2] W. Christ, *Geschichte der griechischen Litteratur* (6th ed.; 1912), p. 73; L. Laistner, *Das Rätsel der Sphinx* (1889).

[3] M. Bréal, in L. Constans, *La Légende d'Oedipe* (1881), p. 4.

[4] Theodor Reik, "Oedipus und die Sphinx," *Imago*, VI (1920), 95–131.

[5] A. Dessenne, *Le Sphinx, étude iconographique* (1957).

sumed, imitations or borrowings of the image that had its birth in Egypt. Neither Greece, nor Asia Minor, nor the islands, nor Assyro-Babylonia, nor Palestine claimed the Sphinx as its own. According to Pisander, the Sphinx came to Thebes in Boeotia from Ethiopia.[6]

The Great Sphinx at Gizeh near Cairo, the largest and most famous since antiquity, has in all ages attracted the attention and aroused the curiosity of travelers, as of almost everyone on earth. It has always been thought that some mystery, some secret or riddle, is embodied in it, and its face, looking with bright open eyes toward the East, wears a smile that bespeaks an eternally enigmatic thought. This Sphinx, cut out of the rock, has survived the longest and is the oldest, dating from the Old Kingdom. Like all sphinxes, it has a human face with an animal body; in this respect a sphinx differs from other images of Egyptian deities which have human bodies and animal heads. The face of the Sphinx at Gizeh is that of Pharaoh Chephren, successor to Cheops; Chephren's pyramid, a little smaller than that of Cheops, is nearby.

The animal body is that of a lion or lioness. The pharaoh was thus represented as a powerful god. In later times many sphinx images were carved, in sculpture and in relief, but smaller in size down to miniature images on cameos, and the face was often that of the reigning monarch. For the most part, the sphinx was depicted in a reclining position, but sometimes it was rampant. During the New Kingdom, under the Eighteenth Dynasty, the Sphinx of Gizeh was called Harmachis, or Hor-em-akhet, "Horus of the Horizon," also "Horus of the Necropolis."[7]

The man who came closer than anyone else before him to

[6] Bethe, *Thebanische Heldenlieder*, p. 21.

[7] S. Hassan, *The Sphinx* (1949), p. 132; idem, *The Great Sphinx and Its Secrets* (1953), p. 240; Dessenne, *Le Sphinx, étude iconographique,* p.176.

solving the "secret" of the Sphinx was the learned Egyptologist, Professor Edouard Naville; in the course of almost five decades (1875–1924) he published several essays dealing with the problem. "The Destruction of Men by the Gods," based on a mythological narrative in the tomb of Pharaoh Seti in Thebes, was an early publication of Naville's pertaining to the subject.[8] The gods delegated the goddess Hathor, in her form as Tefnut or Sekhmet, to punish mercilessly the rebellious people who did not submit to the will of the gods. The text says: "This goddess [Hathor] went out and killed the men on earth. . . . And lo! Sechmet waded with her feet through many nights in their blood, down to the city of Heracleopolis." Naville asked: Must we assume that "destruction of men" concerned "all of humanity"? And he concluded: "This appears evident, because the inscriptions do not speak of some men, but of men, in general."

In 1902–6 Naville, who in the meantime had excavated extensively in Egypt, presented strong arguments based on ancient texts that the Sphinx is an effigy of the goddess Tefnut or of Hathor in her murderous aspect, and the animal body is that of a lioness.[9] Hathor was the feminine personification of Horus, and her name means "The House of Horus." Naville again elaborated on the subject in 1924.[10]

Other scholars, however, believe that the female Sphinx appeared rather suddenly in the reign of Amenhotep III, known as the Magnificent, and his queen Tiy of the Eighteenth Dynasty.[11] Gizeh was the royal necropolis of Memphis, and Memphis was the ancient capital of Lower Egypt; the capital

[8] Edouard Naville, "La Destruction des hommes par les dieux. D'après une inscription mythologique du tombeau de Séti I, à Thèbes," *Transactions of the Society of Biblical Archaeology*, IV (1876), Part I, pp. 1–19.

[9] *Sphinx*, V (1902), 193–99; ibid., X (1906), 138–40; cf. Gardiner, in *Journal of Egyptian Archaeology*, XXXIX (1953), 14, n. 2.

[10] *Sphinx*, XXI (1924), 12–23.

[11] Dessenne, *Le Sphinx, étude iconographique*, p. 107.

of Upper Egypt was Thebes, now Luxor and Karnak, more than three hundred miles to the south. During one of the most illustrious periods of Egyptian history—that of the Eighteenth Dynasty—Thebes was the capital of the entire land, Upper and Lower Egypt.

On the rocks overlooking the city of Thebes and guarding the approaches from the west was a shrine dedicated to Hathor, the goddess that once destroyed humankind. "Hathor presided over the western cliffs of Thebes."[12] The slayer of the human race, who had to be appeased and worshiped lest she repeat the bloodshed, dominated from the precipitous cliffs; behind them was the necropolis of Thebes, the Valley of the Kings.

There was also a temple or chapel dedicated to Hathor. The Hathor of Der el-Medinah was "Hathor who-is-in-the-midst-of-Thebes, the Mistress of the West."[13] She was also "the goddess of the deserts, and at Thebes a form of her, the snake Mersegret, protected the desert tombs."[14] From images preserved in relief we know that there was a Theban Sphinx to whom human sacrifices were made in the Eighteenth Dynasty.

The mythological portion of the Oedipus story may serve as a pathfinder to the land where possibly the legendary motif of the story grew out of some historical happenings. It is actually not the riddle presented by the Sphinx to travelers but the puzzle it is to scholars that may bring us to the gates of the city where evil days befell the king who married his mother.

[12] F. L. Griffith, "Thebes," *Encyclopaedia Britannica*, 14th ed.

[13] W. C. Hayes, in *Journal of Egyptian Archaeology*, XXXIV (1948), 114, n. 3; P. M. Fraser, ibid., XLII (1956), 97.

[14] H. R. Hall (British Museum), "Egypt: Religion," *Encyclopaedia Britannica*, 14th ed. The temple of Mentuhotep V, dedicated to Horus, was situated "on the top of the cliff somewhat to the north of the entrance of the Valley of the Tombs of the Kings." C. F. Nims, "Places about Thebes," *Journal of Near Eastern Studies*, XIV (1955), 111ff.

The Seven-Gated Thebes
and The Hundred-Gated Thebes

THEBES, the ancient capital of Boeotia in Greece, located in rolling country, was once one of the most famous cities of the Hellenes. According to tradition, it was founded by Cadmus, who, coming from the Phoenician coast, brought the art of writing to the Hellenes. With almost no other city in Greece were there so many legends connected as with Thebes. For many centuries it was a city filled with pride in its past, in which all Hellenes participated. Even Hercules' nativity was sometimes placed in Thebes; Hercules tended his flocks on Mount Cithaeron, the same desolate pastural highland between Boeotia and Corinth where, the legend has it, the newborn Oedipus, with his feet pierced, was exposed.

In later, historical times, Thebes made war on Athens and Sparta. Its people supported the cause of the Persians and fought on their side at Thermopylae (–480). When one of the Boeotian towns, Plataea, declared its independence, and Athens supported the seceders, the Thebans became bitter enemies of Athens. And when in the ensuing Peloponnesian War Athens surrendered to Sparta (–404), the Thebans clamored for its destruction.

After the Peloponnesian War Thebes and Sparta entered a period of rivalry for supremacy in Greece. Thebes allied itself with Argos and Athens to defeat Sparta in the Corinthian War (–387); gaining temporary hegemony, Thebes humiliated Sparta. Its authority was established also in Macedonia in the north, and Philip, the youngest son of the Macedonian king, was held as a hostage and raised in Thebes. Later the Thebans invited Philip to participate in the internal struggles of the Greek states, but when he was about to conquer Athens, Thebes, fearing the expansion of the Macedonian state to neighboring Athens, allied herself with this city, and together they suffered defeat at Chaeronea. The Boeotian confederacy was dissolved, and a Macedonian garrison occupied the Theban citadel. When Philip died, Thebes revolted, and the eighteen-year-old Alexander gained his early laurels by storming and taking the city. A congress at Corinth decided to raze Thebes, the cause of many internal wars, and only the house in which two centuries earlier the great poet Pindar had been born was spared by order of Alexander.

This Boeotian city was called the "seven-gated" Thebes because of its outer wall with seven gates and in order to distinguish it from the "hundred-gated" Thebes in Egypt.

The Egyptian city—in Egyptian it was called Ne or No ("Residence") or No-Amon ("Residence of Amon," as in the Hebrew text of the book of the Prophet Nahum 3:8)[1]—did not have an outer wall with a hundred gates in it, but in time of war and siege its vast temple enclosures could form scores of bastions with gates.[2] Luxor and Karnak are parts of this ancient capital on the Nile, as are also Deir el Bahari with the temple of Queen Hatshepsut, the Ramesseum of Ramses II, and Medinet Habu with the temple of Ramses III. These mortuary temples were built in the plain on the western bank of the Nile, below the towering cliffs that concealed the Valley of the Kings,

[1] It was also called "The Southern Residence" and Weset.

[2] Cf. Diodorus, i. 45. 7.

where the remains of the kings were hidden in unmarked cave chambers to protect them from desecration and the treasures entombed with them from being looted. But the mortuary temples built to perpetuate the names of the great pharaohs did not escape the ravages of war and time. Of the mortuary temple of Amenhotep III, the most opulent of the tenants of the throne of Egypt, nothing is left save two enormous statues of the seated king—so large that each finger is three feet long. Of one of them Greek and Roman travelers related that it emitted a musical sound at sunrise. The restoration work performed by order of the Emperor Septimius Severus was held responsible for the cessation of the complaining sighs. These two statues were called Memnon colossi by the Greeks, who thought they were likenesses of Memnon, the dark-skinned warrior who came from a southern country to help the Trojans besieged by the Achaeans. Memnon was killed by Achilles, and the sighs heard when the morning rays of the sun lighted the figure were thought by the Greeks to be Memnon's greeting to his mother, the Dawn. But the statues are of Amenhotep III, and he was not the son of the Dawn.

Ramses II of the Nineteenth Dynasty, who tried to rival Amenhotep III in the size and magnificence of his buildings, made an equally large image of himself before his mortuary temple, about a thousand tons in weight and nearly sixty feet high. But since antiquity it has lain broken with its face in the dust, listening to the guides who daily repeat a string of baseless tales.

The city itself was on the eastern bank of the Nile. Its origin— around the sanctuary of Amon—is lost in antiquity. During the Old Kingdom it was a provincial temple town. In the days of the Middle Kingdom a pharaoh erected his mortuary temple on the west bank. But in the days of the New Kingdom, of the dynasty that replaced the Shepherd-Kings, Thebes became a capital that by the grandeur of its buildings surpassed all capitals of its time. The early kings of the Eighteenth Dynasty and especially the great conqueror, Thutmose III, built the Karnak temple to Amon. Amenhotep III, three generations later, built three new large temples, to Mont, to Mut, and to Amon.

In the seventh century before the present era Assurbanipal, king of Assyria, sacked Thebes, reduced it to ruins, and threw down its statues; but only a few decades later the Assyrian capital, Nineveh, was stormed and burned by the Babylonians and the Medes, and the Prophet Nahum exclaimed: "Nineveh is laid waste: who will bemoan her? . . . Art thou better than populous No, that was situate among the rivers . . . ?" Nineveh did not rise from the ashes, but Thebes did. The Persians superseded the Babylonians, took Babylon, and in the next generation, under Cambyses, reached Egypt. Thebes was once more mercilessly destroyed;[3] the Persian had no fear of or respect for Egyptian gods.

After a great and long struggle the Greeks, led by Alexander of Macedonia, triumphed over the Persians. Alexander reached Egypt; he did not ruin it, he built in it. He did not go as far as Thebes, for he was busy planning a new capital that would bear his own name. After his death Ptolemy, one of Alexander's generals and his governor in Egypt, became king of Egypt; his line expired three hundred years later, after Rome had superseded Greece, when the last of the house of Ptolemy, Cleopatra, heavily involved in the intrigues and war for the succession to power after Caesar's violent death, took her own life in –30. During the two thousand years since the end of the kingdom of Egypt the vast buildings of Thebes have "served as quarries for millstones and for the lime-burners," yet Thebes still presents "the greatest spectacle of monumental ruins remaining from ancient times."

[3] Strabo, xvii. 1. 46. Cf., however, Posener, *La Première Domination perse en Egypte* (1936), p. 171.

The Oedipus legend is connected with Thebes in Boeotia. Thebes in Egypt, known to the Greeks by this name at least since the time of Homer, was the greater of the two; it was also the more ancient.

The New Kingdom was created by the efforts of Kamose and Ahmose, brothers who fought against the waning domination of the Shepherd-Kings; of Thutmose I, who penetrated into Asia, and of his daughter Hatshepsut, who increased and enriched the empire by peaceful intercourse with neighboring nations; of Thutmose III, who undertook a series of military thrusts deep into the Near East and made Egypt greater than ever before or after. Thutmose III was followed by Amenhotep II, a man of great physical strength, cruel and vain, but a far less powerful military commander than his predecessor. When he returned from an unsuccessful campaign to Syria-Palestine, where he went with a force too big to maneuver or to supply adequately, he hanged captured sheikhs head down from the masts of the royal barge that carried him on his triumphant journey along the Nile.

According to his inscriptions, Amenhotep II made human sacrifices to Amon in Thebes by clubbing prisoners before the god. It may be safely assumed that this action took place in front of a statue of a sphinx, for Amenhotep had himself portrayed before a sphinx, the inscription on which explains that it represents Amon. Amenhotep II personally acted in the role of executioner.

This pharaoh's mummy was found together with his bow in the tomb he built for himself in the Valley of the Kings; from his inscriptions it is known that it was his great pride that no other prince or commander had the strength to bend his bow.

In the 1920s a large stele was found in the sand close to the great Sphinx of Gizeh on which Amenhotep II described how he was chosen by the oracle of the Sphinx to be king and how in gratitude he built a chapel for the oracle. It was apparent from this tablet that the priests in the sanctuary of the Sphinx served as oracles in matters of succession. The future monarch had to perform some feats of sportsmanship, such as hunting or driving a chariot, following which he lay down in the sanctuary. "By a mysterious sign or a miraculous voice, of the source of which the Greet Seer of Heliopolis was probably not ignorant, the father of gods dictated to the new monarch the rules of his conduct."[4] B. Bruyère assumed that, in order to compete with the priests of Heliopolis, the priests of Karnak erected a chapel at Thebes where at the feet of the Sphinx oracular prophecies were made: the Sphinx there represented Amon, the father of gods, for oracular purposes.

Amenhotep II was followed on the throne of Egypt by Thutmose IV, not the elder son of the king, but the one whom the oracle had chosen. Not in the line of succession, just one of the princes in the royal household, he was in his late teens when he had an oracular dream. On a hunting expedition in the desert, close to the Sphinx of Gizeh, he stopped to rest in the shadow of the Sphinx, fell asleep, and heard the Sphinx declare to him that he would become king and would repay the oracle by clearing the figure of the Sphinx of the sand of the encroaching desert. He made a vow that he would do this. When he became king he placed a stele, on which he described what had happened to him, between the paws of the Sphinx, where it was found in modern times when once more the Sphinx was cleared of the sand of the desert which had blown through all four seasons of all the centuries. The manner in which the oracle communicated with Thutmose was not uncommon among the famous oracles of ancient times. So, for instance, in Epidaurus in Greece, Asclepius would reveal the remedy to those who sought to be healed while they were asleep.

[4] B. Bruyère, "Le Sphinx de Gizeh et les épreuves sportives du sacre," *Chronique d'Egypte*, XIX (1944), 194–206.

Thutmose became pharaoh, but the oracle had not disclosed to him that he would die while still young. The throne was then occupied by his son, Amenhotep III. The cult of the sphinx was very much in vogue in the days of Amenhotep II and Thutmose IV, who owed the throne to the benevolence of the sphinx which had revealed their destiny to them in dreams, and this cult remained popular in the days of their successor. Not only did it remain in vogue, it became rampant. There was a resurgence of the worship of the sphinx unknown since the Old Kingdom.

A. Dessenne in his monograph, *Le Sphinx, étude iconographique*, describes the metamorphosis of the image of the sphinx in the days of Amenhotep and his wife Tiy. In former times the ruling monarch occasionally had himself represented in the effigy of a sphinx; however, it was usually not Amenhotep but Tiy who was fashioned in the form of a sphinx. Following the long-standing tradition of a male-faced sphinx, Queen Hatshepsut had been sculptured as a sphinx with a beard suspended from the chin. But Tiy had her sphinx made with a woman's face. Furthermore, for the first time female breasts were added to the lion's body of the sphinx: there was no doubt that it became a female. It also had wings, while the Sphinx of Gizeh and other early ones were as a rule wingless. In the past the sphinx had been represented in a lying or standing position, as if motionless, but this was changed in the days of Amenhotep III and Tiy.

Dessenne expressed his wonder: with the feminization of the sphinx one would hardly expect it to become a cruel creature, but this is what happened.[5] Tiy in the form of a winged sphinx with female breasts is shown tearing apart or strangling its victim. This was a new idea in art that "suddenly appeared, without transition."

[5] Dessenne, *Le Sphinx, étude iconographique*, pp. 109, 186.

The cruel winged maiden Sphinx of Boeotian Thebes was not only a guest from the land of the Nile as Pisander in his scholium to Euripides described it, but, more precisely, it was an image that appeared first at Thebes in Egypt in the days of Queen Tiy.

Amenhotep III and Tiy

QUEEN Tiy was a remarkable woman. The young Amenhotep married her at the beginning of his reign. She was not of royal blood, not a foreign princess, but the daughter of a civil servant and provincial priest, Yuya. She was not like other queens before her, completely overshadowed by their royal husbands. In the past there had been a woman on the throne of Egypt—Hatshepsut, about a hundred years earlier—but none of the royal wives ever had such prominence as Tiy.

The marriage of the king to his queen was made an event of historical proportions. Large "marriage seals" or unusually big scarabs engraved with the names of Amenhotep and Tiy were distributed in great numbers throughout Egypt and abroad; they also bore the names of Tiy's parents—she was so certain of her position and authority that there was no attempt to ascribe to her divine descent or royal birth. Other large seals with the names of Amenhotep and Tiy have been discovered in the foundations of public buildings: for instance, in Palestine, in the foundation of the temple at Beth Shemesh. In Mycenae, where Schliemann dug in search of the tomb of Agamemnon, a small Tiy scarab was found.

Amenhotep's royal decrees were published in his name and in that of his queen, a procedure that had no precedent in the Egyptian past. Tiy's portraits are numerous, in sculpture and low relief. They disclose a determined face, not without charm. From her start as a daughter of commoners, Tiy made for herself an unusual career.

She also raised her parents to an exalted position, and when they died they were very well mummified and buried in the Valley of the Kings with rich furniture. Until the discovery of the tomb of Tutankhamen, the rich tomb of Yuya and Tuya, his wife, was a singular find in the necropolises of Egypt; it had never been disturbed;[1] the faces of the dead are unusually well preserved and reveal the traits of these persons, almost their characters.

Above all the builders of Thebes, Amenhotep III distinguished himself by erecting famous structures at Karnak and Luxor, the two great temple areas. In the Karnak temple of Amon (Amen), the chief deity of Egypt, he built the third Karnak pylon; it "displayed the brilliance and magnificence of Imperial Thebes." Amenhotep described the decorations that embellished the structure. Two steles of lapis lazuli, a deep blue stone, were set up, one on each side of the towering gateway. The door was overlaid with gold and inlaid with lapis lazuli and precious stones; the floor was of silver. The flagstaffs fastened to the towers were overlaid with gold so that "they shone more than the heavens." In front of the pylon was erected a colossal statue of the king, twenty cubits high. An avenue of sphinxes led up from the river to the gateway; another avenue of sphinxes led from the Karnak temple to the temple of Luxor, a mile and a half away. This avenue has survived in part to our day.

The temple of Luxor was started and built by Amenhotep III. To the Egyptians it was known as Southern Harim of Amon. It, too, was dedicated to the chief god. It is majestic and beautiful and exquisitely proportioned. It was almost in its en-

[1] The jewels, however, were stolen, probably by the priests who wrapped the mummies.

tirety the work of Amenhotep III, "the Louis XIV of ancient Egypt."[2] In front of this edifice the king constructed a columned hall and a colonnaded forecourt, "the finest in Egypt": "Even in their decay the colonnades still impress one with their beauty, and they form one of the fairest visions ever conjured up by an architect's imagination and materialized by him in enduring stone."[3] Light falling from above played with shadows on sculptured stone pillars in the darkened sanctuary; incense was burned to Amon and his cohorts, and incantations and the muted tones of flute, viol, and harp sounded. Encircling the main sanctuary were sanctuaries of lesser divinities, rooms for special ceremonies, and storerooms for vessels and vestments.

The main ceremony took place in the month of Paophi. The image of Amon was carried from Karnak to Luxor on the sacred barge by more than a score of priests amid rejoicing crowds, and the pharaoh himself participated in the procession. He was looked upon as a descendant of the god, son of Amon himself, and one of his functions, upon arrival at Luxor, was to effect the conception of a next son of Amon, taking upon himself the role of his father Amon and visiting his queen. The paintings on the walls of the temple of Luxor show the conception of the pharaoh by his father Amon and his birth as the son of Amon.

Tiy conceived several times. She gave birth to a son, but of him nothing is known—he was never pictured or mentioned—until he came, on his father's death, to claim the throne. Three daughters of Amenhotep and Tiy lived with their parents and appear on family portraits.

Amenhotep was a passionate hunter. He loved to hunt lions, and he was proud of his record: in the space of ten years he killed one hundred and two lions. These ferocious animals did

[2] A. M. Blackman, *Luxor and Its Temples* (1923), p. 64.
[3] Ibid.

not roam in the valley of the Nile; in order to hunt the royal beasts, the king repeatedly left his capital on extended trips to the deserts and wastes in the outlying regions of his realm, far from human habitations.

The hunting was done from a chariot; bows and arrows and long lances were the weapons. It was a dangerous sport; the wild animal, even more ferocious when wounded, would charge the horses and the hunter, and the frightened steeds might rear or run in a panic off the track and over rocks into a ravine, overturning the chariot and killing the hunter and the chariot-eer.

This hunter of lions was tamed by his wife, Tiy. When the queen expressed displeasure because she was not asked by the priests of Amon to represent the goddess Mut in a festival pageant on the sacred lake of the temple, the king put one hundred thousand men to work,[4] day and night, and in a single fortnight there was excavated an artificial lake, twelve hundred feet wide and over a mile in length, filled with water, planted with lilies, stocked with fish, and encircled with flowering plants, and Tiy surpassed Mut of the priests in the display of extravagance and royal charm.

It was the apogee of imperial Egypt. "The wealth of the known world flowed into Egypt. The harbours of the Delta were crowded with ships of every nationality, loaded with merchandise and with the tribute and presents of subject and friendly states. These ships often, too, it appears, sailed right up the Nile to the Theban docks and there disgorged their cargoes. Furniture overlaid with gold or fashioned of precious woods inlaid with ivory, chariots encrusted with gold and silver, horses of the finest breeds, bronze weapons and armour inlaid

[4] Estimate of R. Engelbach. However, W. C. Hayes, *The Scepter of Egypt*, II, 232, estimates that the task required two hundred and fifty thousand workers. Cf. also a recent paper by J. Yoyotte in *Kêmi*, XV (1959), 23–33.

with gold, gold and silver vessels of rare design, multicoloured and elaborately patterned fabrics, the choicest produce of the fields, gardens, vineyards, orchards, and pastures of Palestine and Syria, incense, sweet-smelling woods, perfumes, silver and gold from Asia and the Sudan—all these were brought in sea-faring ships or by overland caravans to Egypt."[5] This description does not mention everything. Huge, tall trunks of cedar trees from the mountains of Lebanon, pottery from Mycenae, and wild animals from the coast and the interior of Africa, and much more could be added to the list. With this plethora of riches Amenhotep III built temples and palaces and many statues.

As the despot grew older his character became more and more unstable. In a fit of self-indulgence and lasciviousness he "married" one of his daughters, or—which amounts to the same thing—placed her in his private harem.[6] This was scarcely with the blessing of Tiy, the mother of the child; she was a jealous and revengeful woman. And he displayed other strange traits.

Amenhotep the Magnificent, given to luxury and overindulgence, was the only pharaoh who had himself portrayed in female clothes. Pharaohs were never represented in civil dress, much less in female attire. Cyril Aldred, in a recent issue of the *Bulletin* of the Metropolitan Museum of Art (February 1957), reproduced such a sculpture of Amenhotep III and described it thus: "Amenophis [Amenhotep] III in his old age wearing a type of gown usually worn by women." Amenhotep III was married to—or, more correctly, by—a strong-willed woman who climbed to the throne from a family in the ranks of civil servants and who took more royal prerogatives into her hands than any royal wife on the throne of Egypt before or after her. Her hunter-husband, however, was turning his interest to what

[5] Blackman, *Luxor and Its Temples*, pp. 79–80.

[6] Engelbach, in *Annales du service*, XL (1940), 153–57; Varille, ibid. (1941), 651–57.

later was called "Greek love," an inference drawn from the fact that he permitted his artist to portray him dressed as a woman.

More than once the throne of an empire was occupied by an invert. Hadrian, the Roman emperor, made known to all his attachment to Antinous, the Bithynian youth. The emperor journeyed up the Nile to meditate at the feet of the Memnon colossus, not suspecting his own affinity with the prototype of the statue. Incidentally, on this journey Hadrian lost the youth; one day Antinous left the royal yacht and directed a lone oarsman to a spot on the Nile where he left the boat and swam away to be drowned. He apparently took his life as the young Chrysippus did when spoiled by Laius. Hadrian, never comforted, built temples for the dead youth, decreed him to be a god, to worship and celebrate in festivals and to mourn in elegies.

The story of Laius' iniquity sounds strange on Greek soil. Other peoples of antiquity were not free from the sensual inclination ascribed to him, but in Persia, Babylonia, Judea, and Egypt homosexuality was thought of as contemptible. The story of the population of Sodom who, in violation of the laws of hospitality, wished to work their will on Lot's overnight guests, and of the horrible punishment that befell that city and other cities of the plain bears witness both to the ancient existence of the urge and its indulgence and to the moral attitude of the Hebrew penman and his readers, which may reflect, to an admittedly exaggerated degree, the attitude toward this aberration found in the ancient East.

But in Greece in the age of Pericles and in the time of Aeschylus, Sophocles, and Euripides, the fifth century before the present era, love for boys was widespread and not abhorred. "The [Greek] literature of the fifth century is permeated with love for boys, which is also honored by this literature."[7] Before that, in Athens at the end of the seventh and

---

[7] Bethe, *Thebanische Heldenlieder*, p. 144.

the beginning of the sixth centuries, sexual relations between a man and a youth were so general and the people of Athens were so little scandalized by it that Solon, one of the seven wise men of ancient Greece, referred to pederasty as the privilege of a free man.[8]

Before ascribing to their gods this unnatural urge, the Greeks had to come to regard it as respectable. It is true that Homer did not attribute to the warriors of the Achaean host relations that were later called "Greek love," but he tells how the gods abducted the youth Ganymede, with whom, according to many sources, Zeus fell in love. What, then, did the Greek mind find so wrong with Laius, who carried off to his palace the youth Chrysippus, that a curse was put on the king, his wife, and his progeny? Even assuming that the legend originated before the time when Greek love became the custom of the land, it is strange that the authors of later centuries should have imputed to an ancient hero a guilt calling forth such intense displeasure on the part of the gods.

Thus there is a certain incongruity among Greek tragedians, who presented the Laius affair as sinful and his introduction of love between males in Thebes as deserving horrible retribution. This is another argument for regarding the land of the legend's origin as not Greece and the people among whom it originated as not Hellenes.

Like Oedipus, who grew to manhood in a foreign country in the house of Polybus and thought himself to be a son of that king though he was not, the Oedipus legend took literary form in Greece and its hero was thought of as a Greek hero, but it would seem that neither the legend nor its hero was originally Greek.

[8] Plutarch, *Lives*, Solon, 1.

A Stranger on the Throne

T H E final hunting score of Amenhotep III is not known, since
the record breaks off in the eleventh year of his reign and no
further score was written down. After a life of great building
activity, of much diplomatic intercourse and commercial traffic
with the lands of western Asia and the Mediterranean islands,
a silence descends on the end of the hunter-king. History professes not to know whether he died a natural death, was the
victim of a palace intrigue, or failed to return alive from one
of his hunting expeditions. His end was abrupt, as though a
curtain had fallen over Thebes, and when it was raised soon
after, Queen Tiy was the reigning sovereign, alone in charge of
the kingdom. Flinders Petrie early stressed this point: "It appears as if she [Tiy] were sole regent after the death of Amenhotep III and before the active reign of Amenhotep IV [Akh-
naton]."[1]

Akhnaton was a stranger to Thebes and Egypt when he assumed royal power there. He had spent his childhood and
youth abroad, either in Syria or in wandering from country to
country and from court to court in the lands of the Middle
East. His name is never mentioned in the many inscriptions of
Amenhotep III, although of the prince-heir to the throne such
mention would be expected. He and his father are never pic-

[1] W. M. Flinders Petrie, *Tell el-Amarna* (1894), p. 38.

tured together on bas-reliefs;[2] Amenhotep had himself depicted together with his wife and daughters in enormously oversized figures, but no son was ever represented in this or any other family portrait. In the tomb of Yuya and Tuya, parents of Queen Tiy, there were mortuary gifts from the king and queen and their daughters, but none from Akhnaton.[3] Even the mere existence of Akhnaton is nowhere hinted at during the reign of his father, Amenhotep III. Then, after the hunter-king died and his widow Queen Tiy had functioned as the head of the state for a few months or weeks, her son appeared on the scene and took over the rule. It has even been assumed that he usurped the throne.[4]

Among the letters on clay tablets found in the state archives of Tell el-Amarna in the Nile Valley there are letters from a vassal prince or king, Rib-Addi, in Syria-Palestine.[5] He apparently knew Akhnaton from an earlier meeting, and he wrote: "And, behold, the gods and the sun and Baalat of Gubla decreed that thou sit upon the throne of thy father's house in thy land."[6]

About the same time Dushratta, the king of Mitanni, wrote to Akhnaton: "And when my brother Nimmuria [Amenhotep III] died, they proclaimed it, and when they proclaimed I also learned. He was gone . . . and I wept on that day, [and] in the middle of the night I sat; food and wine I did not enjoy on that day and I was grieved. . . . But when Naphuria [Akhnaton], the great son of Nimmuria by Tiy his wife the great one, wrote to me: 'I will enter upon my reign,' I said: 'Nimmuria is not dead.' Now Naphuria, his great son by Tiy, his great wife,

[2] A. Weigall, *The Life and Times of Akhnaton*, p. xx.

[3] T. Davis, *The Tomb of Iouiya and Touiyou* (1907).

[4] Petrie, *Tell el-Amarna*, p. 38.

[5] S. A. B. Mercer, *The Tell el-Amarna Tablets* (1939), I. The identity of Rib-Addi is clarified in *Ages in Chaos*, Vol. I.

[6] Letter 116.

has placed himself in his stead, and he will not change from its place one thing from what it was before. . . . Tiy, his mother, who was the great wife of Nimmuria, the loved one, is alive, and she will report the words to Naphuria, the son of Nimmuria her husband, that we were on excellent friendly terms."[7]

This letter reveals that the passing of Amenhotep III was not made known by his son-heir but by persons described as "they," or the elders of the realm; it also discloses that Akhnaton occupied the throne either on the invitation of the state or following a successful palace revolution; and, finally, it shows that Akhnaton did not know about the relations maintained by his deceased father with foreign rulers and, more specifically, was ignorant of the "excellent friendly terms" that existed between Amenhotep III and the king of Mitanni, relations well known to Queen Tiy.

Dushratta, king of Mitanni, wrote again to Akhnaton: "And all the words which I have spoken with thy father, thy mother, Tiy, knows them. No one else knows them. But thou mayest ask thy mother Tiy about them. Let her tell thee how thy father was on friendly terms with me."[8]

[7] Mercer, *The Tell el-Amarna Tablets*, Letter 29.

[8] Ibid., Letter 28. In order to resolve a series of difficult situations, with which we shall deal later, several scholars have assumed a period of co-regency shared by Akhnaton and his father Amenhotep III, that lasted as long as ten years or more. In the 1957 issue of the *Journal of Egyptian Archaeology*, Sir Alan H. Gardiner wrote of the co-regency as "a controversial issue on which I have, I confess, strong views." He found it "strange" that the supporters of the view make "only passing and irrelevant reference to the el-Amarna letters, to my mind far better historical evidence than the highly ambiguous pictures on tomb-walls. A letter from the Hittite king Suppiluliuma and others from Tushratta, king of Mitanni, show that Akhenaten succeeded only after the death of his father and when he himself was but a mere youth. . . . A letter to Queen Tiye (26, by Tushratta) without explicitly referring to Amenophis III's death, cannot be rationally understood except on the assumption that she was a widow, for she is there urged to impress upon the mind of her son Naphurria, i.e. the later Akhenaten, the good relations which had subsisted between his father and Tushratta. What appears to have been the first letter from the Mitannian

Such unfamiliarity on the part of the heir to the throne implies clearly that Akhnaton was not in Thebes during the years that preceded his father's death; it is inconceivable that a hereditary prince would be completely ignorant of the friendly relations between his father and the king of Mitanni, one of the great kings of that time.

If these circumstances are compared with those of the Oedipus legend, we see that Akhnaton, like Oedipus, spent his childhood and youth abroad; that upon the death of his father, the latter's widow, Tiy, ruled alone as Jocasta did upon the death of her husband, Laius; that after a while Akhnaton occupied the throne, ignorant of state affairs as they had been under his father but knowing that Tiy was his mother and the deceased king was his sire.

Thus, if we are bent on finding a close resemblance between the legendary Oedipus and the historical Akhnaton, we must admit at this point that the evidence does not appear convincing nor the case strong, and woefully inadequate they are. A hero who, when a newborn infant, was left with his feet pierced in a wasteland, and who when grown up killed his father in an encounter on a road[9] and married his mother and had children

king to Naphurria [Akhnaton] (27), bearing a hieratic docket dated in the latter's second year and stating that he was then residing in the Southern City (i.e. Thebes), twice mentions 'the celebration of mourning,' which can surely refer only to Amenophis III's funeral. . . ."

These are the very same arguments I have used in this discourse to rebut the hypothesis of co-regency. If Akhnaton was co-ruler with his father for any length of time, then the correspondence with the Oedipus story is completely shattered.

Clearly against co-regency stands also the fact that early in his reign, before his move to el-Amarna, Akhnaton mutilated the name of his father on all inscriptions, a deed unthinkable during a co-regency.

[9] Constans, *La Légende d'Oedipe*, p. 5, and Nilsson, *The Mycenaean Origin of Greek Mythology*, assume that the murder of the father was a later interpolation in the legend. Nilsson writes: "The slaying of his father is not so essential for the myth and may have been added later" (p. 106).

with her is very different from the customary image of Akhnaton as model husband and son and a religious reformer. If all that we can show is that he spent his youth away from Thebes and that he took over the kingdom after his mother ruled for a short time alone, then we are trying to build an edifice on a few haulms of straw or to buy a kingdom with a few silver coins. Did not the maiden, the clearly mythical Sphinx, direct us to the wrong Thebes? Should we not have clung to Thebes in Boeotia and paid no attention to this episode, obviously interpolated, of a Sphinx on a cliff overlooking the approaches to the seven-gated city? Did Akhnaton marry his mother? Did she bear him children? What about this physical sign that gave Oedipus his name, his swollen feet? And the blindness and exile?

In the Greek legend, the king who lived in incest with his mother was called "swellfoot," Oedipus. The pictures on the walls of Akhet-Aton (Tell el-Amarna) sepulchers and on the boundary stelae of the city show King Akhnaton and the members of his family. These pictures are very different from the pictorial art of Egypt of earlier generations and of later ones. Especially unusual, and even unprecedented, is the handling of the body of Akhnaton. His head is long, his neck is thin, his abdomen is pendulous, but the most pronounced malformation is in the shape of his thighs: they are swollen.

James Breasted wrote: "The strange treatment of the lower limbs by Akhnaton's artists is a problem which still remains unsolved and cannot be wholly accounted for by supposing a malformation of the king's own limbs."[10] But no mannerism in art could be held responsible for the grotesquely enlarged thighs of the king. One of the peculiarities of Akhnaton's body, the extreme elongation of the skull, is characteristic also of the

[10] J. H. Breasted, A History of Egypt (1912), p. 378.

heads of his children, as shown on bas-reliefs and sculptures, but the swollen state of Akhnaton's lower limbs is peculiar to him alone and is repeated in all his very numerous full-length portraits at Thebes and at el-Amarna. The anomaly is so unusual that Breasted thought it could not have been a "natural" malformation.

In the *Revue Neurologique* for 1920, two French physicians, Drs. M. Ameline and P. Quercy, published a paper, "Le Pharaon Amenophis IV, sa mentalité. Fut-il atteint de Lipodystrophie Progressive?" G. Elliot Smith, professor of anatomy at the University of London and author of books on Egyptian royal mummies, most of which he opened and examined, thus reported on this "very curious memoir": "They describe the condition of progressive lipodystrophy as an affection characterized on the one hand by a progressive and complete disappearance of the subcutaneous fat of the upper part of the body; and, on the other, by a marked increase of the adipose tissue below the loins. The first example of this strange affection was described by Barraquer in 1907, but it is exceedingly rare in adult men."[11]

This disproportion in the bodily build, with the lower part of the body swollen while the upper part is lean, is very rare in our time, and it must have been rare also in the past. One afflicted with this condition would scarcely expose himself to public view or pose in the nude. But Akhnaton was different. A king of the greatest realm of his time, he wished to impress on his subjects and their descendants that his deformity was a sign that he was an elect of destiny and a divine being himself. Whatever the medical diagnosis of the bodily deformity and of the psychological attitude, Akhnaton, by means of his public appearances while scantily clothed and his numerous nude

[11] G. Elliot Smith, *Tutankhamen and the Discovery of His Tomb* (1923), pp. 85–88.

statues, must have made his physical defect a matter of common knowledge. This new aesthetics of the outlines of the human body, imposed on royal sculptors as a thing to emphasize and not to hide, was unappreciated by the Egyptians, accustomed as they were in their art to the charm of a well-proportioned body, illustrated in numerous scenes of the hunt, music, and the dance from many centuries of the Egyptian past.

The malformation or deformity of Akhnaton's legs appears grotesque to a modern spectator; in antiquity it must have struck the onlooker at his bas-reliefs and statues in the same way.

In the legend Oedipus' feet are swollen; in the pictures of Akhnaton the thighs are swollen. In folklore feet may stand for legs. Many languages do not have different words for legs and feet. In Greek, the word *pous* stands for both; in Egyptian, too, the word *r-d* (foot) stands also for leg.[12] In the riddle that Oedipus solved concerning the creature that walks on four legs, on two, and on three (the staff being the third), the Greek word used is *pous*, and thus the name Oedipus could, and even preferably so, mean "swollen legs."

The body of Akhnaton has never been discovered, but the skeletal remains of his two sons, as we shall see, have been. The cranial malformations depicted in the portraits of these princes were confirmed in the skeletons. This is evidence that the sculptures and pictures of Akhnaton's body are truthful representations as far as his swollen legs are concerned.

King Akhnaton and the entire royal family, in a continuous spectacle of exhibitionism, used to appear in public almost nude; at least so they were shown on the bas-reliefs, surrounded by a crowd of their subjects. At the sight of such a malformation, a contemporary visitor from Mycenaean Greece might con-

12 In Hebrew, as well, *regel* is the lower limb and likewise the foot. In Russian also the same word (*noga*) is used for both.

ceivably have given the king the agnomen Oedipus.[13] Later, when a Greek could know of the king and his misshapen body only from surviving sculptures, the same impression must have been received on contemplating the royal likenesses.

As for the legend of Oedipus, some students of classical lore have wondered at the additional cruelty inflicted on the exposed infant by piercing his feet. An explanation has been offered according to which this measure was intended to prevent the spirit of the child, when he died, from walking about. Several competent scholars, however, have expressed the belief that the piercing of the feet was a later interpolation and that the original legend did not have this element.[14]

Professor Gardiner of Oxford asked, What is the meaning of the *epitheton constans*, or the regular epithet that Akhnaton applied to himself, "Who lived long" [or better, "Who survived to live long"], and this even on his earliest monuments? Why should a young man have expressed himself that way? What could have been the original meaning of this appellation? Gardiner wondered. "Is it possible that in youth Akhenaten was not expected to live long?"[15]

The Oedipus legend provides us with a possible answer: Oedipus was destined to die when a baby, but he survived. The miracle of survival was all-decisive in the life of the legendary hero. The miraculous survival of an infant, imperiled by a father, a pharaoh, or a Herod, but destined to grow to be

---

[13] The second part of the name Amen-hotep (IV) also might possibly contribute to the name Oedipus. The Egyptian letter *t* is found transcribed in personal names as *d* in cuneiform (el-Amarna letters). For instance, Tutu, the royal Minister for Foreign Affairs under Akhnaton, whose name thus appears in his tomb in el-Amarna, is addressed as Dudu in the el-Amarna letters.

[14] Kretschmer, *Griechische Vaseninschriften*, p. 191, n. 3 p. (1894); idem, *Glotta*, XII (1923), 59f.

[15] A. H. Gardiner, "The So-Called Tomb of Queen Tiye," *Journal of Egyptian Archaeology*, XLIII (1957), 21, n. 3.

a hero, is thought by critics like Lord Raglan to be a stereotype of a story attached to practically all biographies of legendary heroes. However, the ever recurring appellation, "Who survived to live long," used by Akhnaton, may signify, if we should be able to substantiate our main thesis, that this element in the story of the newly born Oedipus is an echo of a true event.

In this connection it may be significant that during the Eighteenth Dynasty in Egypt, the dynasty to which Amenhotep III and Akhnaton belonged, it was, as already said on a previous page, usual to inquire of the oracle as to the royal succession. Such was not the case with the earlier dynasties, nor was this role of the oracle in matters of royal succession evident in later times; but during the Eighteenth Dynasty and, more precisely, during the second half of the dynasty, the oracle was repeatedly consulted by the pharaohs to learn the dynastic succession and generally to hear what was in store for the king and his progeny. This, of course, gave the priests of the oracle unusual power. In the days of Amenhotep III the oracle at Heliopolis at the apex of the delta in the temple of the god Ra and the oracle at Gizeh declined from their former prominence, and the oracle of Thebes grew in influence. Thebes being the capital of Upper and Lower Egypt during the Eighteenth Dynasty, the priests of Amon of the great Karnak temple there actually dominated the monarchy. It is quite certain that Amenhotep III inquired of the oracle of Amon in Thebes about the succession, possibly even before his son was born. The circumstance that Akhnaton was reared away from Thebes and outside Egypt must have had some relation to the utterance of the oracle, otherwise why should a royal son, destined to inherit the crown, grow up in a foreign land? The expression, "Who survived to live long," indicates that Akhnaton was in danger of dying early in life. Consequently we may infer that the oracle was of such an unpropitious nature that the boy must have been removed, possibly to be destroyed. His being sent away, conceivably to the house of the Mitanni relatives of Amenhotep III, could have been in substitution for the killing of the child, and this could have been done, it appears, only if a holy man, like the seer Tiresias of the Greek legend, intervened and gave this advice. On a later page we shall be able to establish the identity of this blind seer.

With this reconstruction of events surrounding the early life of Akhnaton we may better understand his animosity toward the priests of Amon and Amon himself and also the early source of his future reform. He was hostile to the entire hierarchy that dominated Thebes and the kingdom. He actually destroyed the oracle of Thebes; nothing is heard of it in his day.

Since the oracle of Heliopolis (On, in Egyptian) was as ancient as the oracle of Thebes, or even older, one would expect that Akhnaton would have secured for himself the benevolence of the oracle of Heliopolis and of its priests. And in fact, after several years on the throne, upon leaving Thebes for el-Amarna, he surrounded himself with the priests from Heliopolis, as the inscriptions of el-Amarna inform us.

But even before that the dominance of the Sphinx in Thebes had ceased. The image was destroyed. It probably was toppled from the western cliff. At the bottom of the cliff, not far from the temple of Hatshepsut, many fragments of sphinxes were found.[16] It is even possible that the priests of the Hathor sanctuary toppled it themselves to save their own lives, for the oracle of Thebes was affiliated with the Sphinx of Thebes, as the oracle of On was affiliated with the Sphinx of Gizeh, and the oracle of Thebes may have laid the doom of death on Akhnaton, a fate he miraculously escaped.

Figures of sphinxes and of the former king as well were mutilated and defaced. There is a case of a stele described by Selim Hassan, at present in charge of the Cairo Museum. "These

[16] *Bulletin of the Metropolitan Museum of Art*, section II, February 1928, p. 46, figs. 48, 51.

sphinxes have been systematically erased, only their outlines remain to show what was originally there. Before each sphinx was a standing figure of the king, which has also suffered erasure . . . those are clearly the erasures made by the iconoclasts of Akhenaton."[17]

The Sphinx, the cruel winged maiden on the cliff at the approaches to Thebes, watching over the city, reappeared in the legend of Oedipus; only there its presence is not motivated. Why should there have been on the cliffs of Thebes in Boeotia a sphinx that destroyed wayfarers? And why should it have thrown itself from the cliff because of an exchange of question and answer? Bloody monsters do not kill themselves in chagrin over a riddle that has been correctly solved and they do not voluntarily cast themselves from a cliff.

[17] S. Hassan, *Annales du Service*, XXXVIII, 57.

"King Living in Truth"

SOMETIME after ascending the throne Amenhotep IV changed his name to Akhnaton. This action was a consequence of his religious reform of replacing the supreme god Amon by the god Aton. The usual interpretation has it that Amon-Ra was the sun god and that Aton was also the sun god, but in a different aspect: the solar disk, or the material substance of the sun. These theological subtleties on the part of modern scholars, who ascribe them to the ancient Egyptians and see in the change a great religious reform, are not convincing. Anyway, Amon was not a solar deity, and besides, there was an idea and a philosophy of life and an ethical concept in Akhnaton's reform.

Amon was the same as Jupiter, worshiped by all the nations of antiquity. In Greece his name was Zeus; in Babylonia, Marduk; and, as we intend to demonstrate in another work, it was Mazda in Persia and Siwa in India. We actually have the testimony of classical authors that Amon was Jupiter, and the famous sacrarium in the Siwa Oasis in the Libyan desert to which Alexander of Macedonia made his pilgrimage in −332 was said by Greek authors to have been dedicated to Zeus-Ammon and by Latin authors to Jupiter-Ammon.[1]

On many bas-reliefs Akhnaton is pictured under rays that

[1] Plutarch, *Lives*, Alexander, 27.

spread out from a disk and end in the form of hands holding the sign of life. In a hymn to Aton by Akhnaton or by his royal poet, found inscribed on the wall of a mausoleum intended for a man by the name of Ay, of whom more later, a fervent longing for union with the deity is expressed in beautiful phrases, in the manner of the Hebrew Psalms.[2]

> Thy rays, they encompass the lands . . .
> Thou bindest [men] by thy love,
> Though thou art afar, thy rays are on earth. . . .
> When thou sendest forth thy rays . . .
> All trees and plants flourish,
> The birds flutter
> Their wings uplifted in adoration of thee. . . .
> Thou art he who createst the man-child in woman,
> Who makest seed in man,
> O thou sole god, whose powers no other possesseth. . . .
>
> Thou makest the beauty of form, through thyself alone. . . .
> Thou art in my heart,
> There is no other that knoweth thee,
> Save thy son Akhnaton.
> Thou hast made him wise in thy designs
> And in thy might . . .
> For thou art duration. . . .
> By thee man liveth,
> And their eyes look upon thy beauty. . . .
> Since thou didst establish the earth,
> Thou hast raised them up [they live] for thy son
> Who came forth from thy limbs,
> The King living in truth. . . .

"Living in truth" is an expression that Akhnaton took as his personal agnomen, and wherever "living in truth" is found, even when the name of the king on an inscription has been

[2] The great similarity of certain passages in this poem to Psalm 104 has been noticed and much reflected upon. Parallel texts can be found in Breasted, A History of Egypt, p. 371–76.

destroyed, it is concluded that the person meant is Akhnaton.

There can be no question that in this personal relation between a man and his god there was something new, something that had not been experienced previously in the same degree in the religion of Egypt, or at least had not been documented by an earlier or later hymn, prayer, or litany.[3] It cannot be overlooked that Akhnaton regarded himself as the crown of creation; he alone knew the Creator; all men live for "thy son."

The religious reform of Akhnaton has been the subject of a great number of books and essays. James Breasted, the Egyptologist, called Akhnaton "the world's first idealist and the world's first individual," "the first prophet of history," and "the most remarkable of all pharaohs and the first individual in human history."[4] Arthur Weigall, also an Egyptologist, echoed these words: "Akhnaton may be ranked in degree of time and . . . perhaps also in degree of genius, as the world's first idealist."[5] Comparisons with Christ are not lacking. But some scholars, certainly in the minority, disagree. So Professor T. E. Peet wrote: "What precisely was the nature of Disk worship as conceived by Akhnaton? This is a subject on which a considerable amount of nonsense has been talked and written, mainly because romance and imagination have been suffered to play too great a part in the inquiry. . . . In the form of the god there is certainly nothing to lend colour to the oft stated belief that the Aten is not the sun's physical disk but 'the power which lay behind it.' On the contrary it may be said that no Egyptian god had ever been represented under so purely physical an aspect as this, even the nature gods having been given a human body. The very word Aten itself tells the same story for it was simply the common Egyptian word for the sun's

[3] However, it was noted that in a hymn to Amon from the time of Amenhotep III there were already expressions of a similar character.

[4] Breasted, A History of Egypt, p. 356.

[5] Weigall, The Life and Times of Akhnaton, p. 2.

disk in the purely material sense, and if there was any real change in Akhenaten's new conception of the sun god as shown in form and name it was in the direction of greater materialism."[6]

We would do an injustice to Akhnaton if we denied that he had an unusually strong feeling for nature and all her creatures. He wrote in his hymn to the sun:

> The chick in the egg that peepeth in
> the shell,
> Thou giveth breath to him within it
> to maintain him;
> Thou has prepared for him his time
> to break his way from the egg,
> And he cometh forth from the egg
> to peep at his time,
> And so he walketh upon his feet. . . .[7]

He did not describe himself as ferocious and vengeful, the way other pharaohs liked to do.

He had the feeling of being the chosen, an only son of the god, for whom the entire world was created. In the days of Amenhotep II, Thutmose IV, and Amenhotep III, human sacrifices were made and the death penalty was meted out. Akhnaton stopped human sacrifices; not even animals were hunted for pleasure. Whereas Amenhotep III boasted of having killed scores of lions, and the pictures of the Theban necropolis show hunting scenes and scenes of birds being wounded or killed with a throwing stick and fish being harpooned, the pictures of the el-Amarna necropolis built under Akhnaton show only peaceful scenes of animal life. There is no known picture of Akhnaton as a hunter and none of him as an executioner; no hunting scene is depicted in the grave-tombs of

[6] T. E. Peet, "Akhenaten, Ty, Nefertete, and Mutnezemt," in W. Brunion, *Kings and Queens of Ancient Egypt* (1925), p. 95.

[7] Trans. G. Steindorff.

65

his nobles; yet he was not a vegetarian, as the pictures of his banquets reveal. He did not have himself represented in war as shooting down rows of his enemies with his bow, as did his predecessors and those who followed him on the throne of Egypt.

Akhnaton freed Thebes of human sacrifices, toppled the Sphinx, and instituted a religion of love—but also of self-adoration.

He chiseled away the name of the god Amon wherever he found it, including its appearances in the name of his father, Amenhotep. He was apparently angry and vengeful against the god, whose oracle was the cause of his ban from the royal house, and against his father who, following the oracle, removed him from the palace. His attitude can be implied from the fact that he did not destroy the god's name in his own name, Amenhotep, which he used till his fourth or fifth year on the throne; neither did he destroy the name Amon in the theophoric name of King Amenhotep I. "The king retained the name of Amenophis [Amenhotep] till the middle of his fifth year, and it is entertaining to see that the 'Amen' of the name remains uninjured in this and all other tombs of the Atenists, though they expunged it from the name of the king's father."[8] Thus the usual explanation that erasing the name of Amon was nothing but the religious zeal of a devotee of Aton is not true. Although he did not erase the name Amon in his own name from his early inscriptions, he changed his name and henceforth called himself Akhnaton instead of Amenhotep.

One of the earlier followers of Freud, recognized by him as the most talented among them, was Karl Abraham; he died early, and therefore his name is not so well known as the names of some of Freud's other pupils. To the first volume of *Imago*,

[8] N. de Garis Davies, "Akhenaten at Thebes," *Journal of Egyptian Archaeology*, IX (1923), p. 139, n. 2.

THE SPHINX OF GIZEH

A SPHINX AT THE FOOT OF THE WESTERN CLIFFS OF THEBES

QUEEN TIY AS A WINGED SPHINX. A CARNELIAN CAMEO. (*Metropolitan Museum of Art*)

"ROYAL WIFE" TIY AS SPHINX. AKHNATON'S NAME IS ERASED. (*Berlin Museum*)

THE "MEMNON COLOSSI." (*Western plain of Thebes*)

COLUMNS OF THE TEMPLE AT LUXOR BUILT BY AMENHOTEP III

AMENHOTEP III IN A CHARIOT. *(Cairo Museum)*

QUEEN TIY. *(Berlin Museum)*

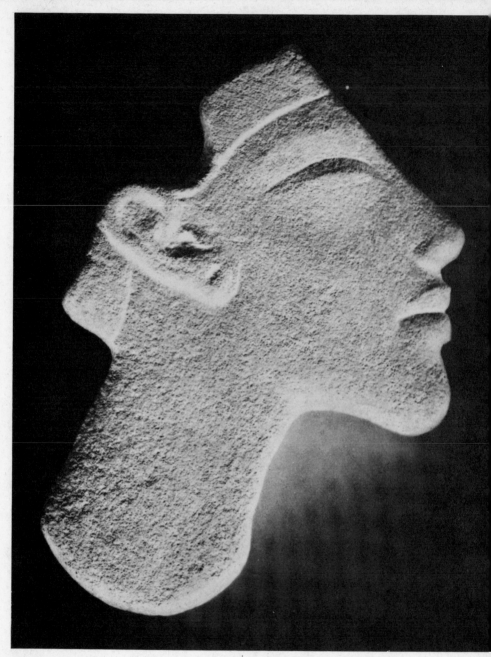

AKHNATON—AS A YOUNG KING. *(Berlin Museum)*

published by Freud in 1912, Abraham contributed an essay, "Amenhotep IV [Akhnaton]." He recognized in the heretical pharaoh a hostility toward his father and an equally strong attachment to his mother.

Abraham followed the erroneous chronological scheme according to which Akhnaton came to the throne at the age of ten. The error arose from the fact that a mummy of a prince about twenty-four years old at his death, but certainly not older than twenty-seven, was mistakenly thought to be Akhnaton; and since Akhnaton reigned for about seventeen years it was concluded that he became king at the age of ten. Following the same scheme, it would have to be concluded that Akhnaton made his break with the cult of Amon at the age of fourteen and soon thereafter wrote the quoted hymn, which was also considered rather perplexingly precocious.

Abraham assumed that a ten-year-old boy coming to the throne would be dominated by his mother. "His libido became fixed in an unusually strong degree on his mother, and his attitude towards his [deceased] father became equally strongly negative."

In Akhnaton's religious reform Dr. Abraham saw a rebellion against the father or, more properly, against the memory of the father. Akhnaton mutilated the name of his father in all inscriptions that he could lay his hand on; he also erased the name of the god Amon and turned to the worship of Aton. It was generally thought and still is that this erasure of the name of the deity was the consequence of religious zeal and nothing else. But Abraham held that the name of Amon was hateful to the young king because it was contained in the name of his father, Amenhotep. "He had the name of Amon and the name of his father, Amenhotep, obliterated on all inscriptions and monuments." In this "purifying" action, as well as in the change of his own name from Amenhotep to Akhnaton, the hidden hatred of the son for his father came to light. "His strongest hatred was directed against his father whom he could not reach because he was no more among the living." By destroying his father's name, the king tried to erase the memory of his sire. By destroying a person's name, his *ka*, or soul in afterlife, was also delivered to destruction.

When Tiy died Akhnaton did not entomb her next to her husband. "The rivalry with his father for the possession of his mother endured beyond death. . . ."

In Abraham's opinion Akhnaton's monotheism was but a sublimation of his hatred. In the place of his father he worshiped the sun, the sole luminary of the daytime sky. "He made Aten the only god in a transparent association with his father. . . ." His religious reform was rooted in his negation of his parent; in his stead he created a sublime ideal of power. He called himself "the son of Aten," thus denying his true origin.

Whatever the true and hidden source of Akhnaton's religious innovations, Abraham, too, thought him a great reformer and prophet. Under Akhnaton, gods were not pictured in animal forms, neither were gods in human figures worshiped. "He was thus a forerunner of Mosaic monotheism," and to an even greater degree he was a forerunner of Christ: "Akhnaton's idea of god is closer to the Christian concept than to the Mosaic."[9] In this evaluation Abraham anticipated Freud.

(The chronological truth is, as I have elucidated in the extensive material contained in *Ages in Chaos*, that Akhnaton was not a teacher of Moses nor his contemporary, but of a much later generation.)

Abraham clearly saw the Oedipus urge in Akhnaton, yet he thought that Akhnaton lived in a monogamous marriage with his queen Nefretete and that the urge was only an urge. He

[9] *Imago*, I (1912), 346–47. The last quotation is Abraham's formulation of Weigall's opinion.

A translation of Abraham's paper was published in the *Psychoanalytical Quarterly*, IV (1935), 537–69.

did not recognize that Akhnaton not only suffered from the Oedipus complex but was the prototype of Oedipus himself. Not only did Akhnaton desire his mother, as so many neurotics do, but he possessed her too. This we are going to establish on succeeding pages. If we are correct, Akhnaton's story is the story of Oedipus himself.

In the fourth year of Akhnaton's reign he definitely broke with the priests of Amon. It was a violent rift. Possibly the oracle made some prediction unfavorable to the king, as some scholars assume.[10] An inscription which he composed for a stele in the place surveyed for his new capital, presently in a damaged condition, reads:

"For, as Father Hor-Aton liveth——more evil are they than those things which I heard unto year four, more evil are they than those things which I have heard in the year——more evil are they than those things which king——heard. . . ."

Monarchy and theocracy clashed. Akhnaton decided to complete the break and return Thebes to what it had been before the New Kingdom and the rise of Amon as the chief god.

The stifling atmosphere of a predominantly hieratic city, with eight great temples of Amon closed, its clergy debased, the nobles of the former reign removed from their positions, made the days in Thebes cheerless. There was nothing sacred for Akhnaton in Thebes: the most sacred thing for an Egyptian king, a memorial tablet of his father, he brutally effaced. This was equal to murder, because in the opinion of the Egyptians the human soul might live after death but not necessarily, and not in all circumstances was it an immortal life. After a man died his mouth had to be opened in a special procedure, with tools designed for that purpose, in order to free his soul and kindle it for a new life; but by destroying a name and a memo-

[10] N. de Garis Davies, *The Rock Tombs of el-Amarna* (1903–8), V, 30–31.

rial, one could rob the dead person of his eternity: "In Ancient Egypt to destroy a person's name was to destroy him himself" (Gardiner). Therefore what Akhnaton did to his father was in the eyes of the Egyptians equal to murder, or even worse: a murdered man could be recalled to life in the Fields of Bliss, but if he was killed there by an action on earth, he had no further existence.

This sacrilege against his heavenly father and his earthly parent could have provoked an oracular word in which the king was condemned as a patricide. Most probably, he referred to this condemnation, when he spoke of the evil things he heard from evil priests in his fourth year which induced him to abandon his capital, Thebes, break completely with the cult of Amon, and look for a site for a new capital, from which the priests of Amon should be barred. His new temple of Aton in Thebes was left behind, the great palaces of the capital were closed, and the young king turned his face northward, nearer to Heliopolis, the ancient On, whose priests and seers regarded themselves as reduced in position and considered that their possessions had been infringed by the cult of Amon, which had been dominant for only a few generations.

Akhnaton did not even acknowledge that he was a son of Amenhotep III. If Tiy had not been referred to as his mother, and several letters of the el-Amarna correspondence had not referred to him as the son of Nimmuria (a spoiled form of Nebmare or Nebmaatre), his relationship to Amenhotep III would not have been known, only guessed. He never called himself "son of Amenhotep" or "son of Nebmare." The first name he erased wherever it was found, and the second name he appropriated to himself, though he wrote it differently. This name he cherished because it contains the word "truth," which he made the heraldic motto of his life. Next to his name he usually wrote "living in truth," *ankh-em-Maat.*

Other cases are known in ancient history of a son adding the name of a deceased father to his own. But in Akhnaton's case it was not filial piety; on the contrary, Akhnaton negated his true origin by claiming that the sun was his father. He was the son of the sun.

"The King of South and North, who liveth in Truth, Lord of the Two Lands, the Son of the Sun, who liveth in Truth, Lord of Diadems, Akhnaton, great in his duration." Aton, the sun, "embraces his Son, his beloved, a Son of Eternity."[11]

In this connection it is interesting that Oedipus, whose parentage is regularly ascribed to Laius, is also called in some ancient sources the son of Helios (sun).[12] Oedipus' descent from Laius is a vital element in the legend; such an unmotivated change in the parentage of the legendary hero seems strange but is understandable if the prototype of the legendary hero was Akhnaton.

A royal son and descendant of the god Ra, like other pharaohs before him, his claim to divinity soon demanded an equality with his heavenly father, Aton, the sun.

"Thou art to eternity like the Aten, beautiful like the Aten who gave him being, Nefer-kheperu-ra [Akhnaton], who fashions mankind and gives existence to generations. He is fixed as the heaven in which Aten is."[13] So wrote his Foreign Minister in a panegyric to the king.

Next Akhnaton insisted that he had created himself, like Ra. Of Ra-Amon it was said he was "husband of his mother." The "favorite concrete expression for a self-existent or self-created

[11] Ibid., p. 16.

[12] "Auch ein Helios wurde als Vater des Oedipus genannt." L. W. Daly, in Pauly-Wissowa, Real-Encyclopädie der classischen Altertumswissenschaft, article "Oedipus," Vol. XVII, Col. 2108. Cf. also W. H. Roscher, Ausführliches Lexikon der griechischen und römischen Mythologie, article "Oedipus" by O. Höfer, Vol. III, Cols. 703, 708.

[13] The Tomb of Tutu (Davies, The Rock Tombs of el-Amarna, VI, 13).

being [was] 'husband of his mother.'"[14] He claimed to be Ra-Aton, and in this spirit he also took over his father's name, Nebmare (Nebmaatre), as if he was himself his own father.

[14] W. M. Flinders Petrie, *Egyptian Tales* (XVIII–XIX Dynasties) (1895), pp. 125–26. More properly translated "bull of his mother."

The City of the Sun

IN THE fifth year of his reign Akhnaton removed his residence from Thebes, the seat of the high priest of Amon at the temple of Karnak, to the new capital, Akhet-Aton. The name of the new capital meant "The place where Aton rises," and was pronounced almost identically with the king's own newly adopted name. He had chosen the site for this city halfway between Thebes and Memphis, downstream on the eastern bank of the Nile. The cliffs of the highland of the eastern desert recede from the river, leaving a lowland area about eight miles long and three miles wide. Here and there ravines of dry wadis cut through the cliffs, a few times a year carrying the water of cloudbursts over the desert that stretches to the Red Sea.

Akhnaton had steles carved in the rock of the cliffs, on the south, north, and east, as boundary marks:

"As my father the Aten liveth, I will make Akhetaten for the Aten my father in this place. I will not make for him Akhetaten south of it, north of it, west of it, or east of it. . . . And the area within these four stelae is Akhetaten in its proper self: it belongs to Aten the father; mountains, deserts, meadows, islands, upper and lower ground, land, water, villages, men, beasts and all things which the Aten my father shall bring into existence eternally forever. I will not neglect this oath which I have made to the Aten my father eternally forever."[1]

[1] This quotation is made up of excerpts from the texts of the steles by Pendlebury, *Tell el-Amarna* (1935), p. v. Complete texts of the steles are in Davies, *The Rock Tombs of el-Amarna*, V.

More steles were placed on the western bank of the Nile, encompassing a large area of fertile fields for tillage and pasture. In a matter of a few years a city rose on the eastern bank; building went on at a feverish pace. Since the limestone of the nearby cliffs proved to be of inferior quality, porous and crumbling, the city in the main was built with bricks of mud but the more important buildings were faced with stone.

A large capital city, stretching for five miles, was surveyed and built. Akhnaton erected palaces and homes for his favorites and sepulchral chambers for himself and for them, for the life hereafter was of as intense concern to the worshipers of Aton as to the worshipers of Amon.

Great thoroughfares running from north to south, paralleling the Nile, were laid out. In the southern part of the city the King's Way passed a pleasure palace of the pharaoh, Maru-Aton; its pavilions had gaily painted walls and floors, and there was a lake, pictures of which show it stocked with fish, rich in reeds and lotuses and water fowl. Running a great distance to the north, the King's Way passed between the Royal House and the State Palace. This palace, area for area, was the largest secular building known from the ancient world. It had a frontage of 700 meters (2200 feet) facing the King's Way. Between the Royal House and the State Palace an arched viaduct spanned the road, and there, probably, was the Window of Appearance at which the pharaoh used to appear before his subjects and from which he showered royal gifts on his favorites.

East of the King's Way and parallel with it stretched the High Priest Road with the estates of the nobles, and still farther to the east was the East Road; all these main arteries were connected by many streets running at right angles to them.

North of the State Palace lay the Great Temple of the Sun's Disk, and east of the palace the Small Temple (Hat Aton). Here, it was decreed, would be the center of the new cult. Not far away, in Official Quarters, were the Hall of Foreign Tribute, the Royal Magazines, the Taxation Offices, the Royal Estate, the Foreign Office, and the Archives, or the "Place of the Correspondence of the King," according to the stamp borne on its bricks. Nearby was the Academy—"House of Life"— where scribes were trained for their future jobs and officers were taught the art of administration. Priests' houses were near the temple, and clerks' dwellings near their offices. Farther to the east were stores, police quarters, armories, a parade ground, cobbled stables, and the station of the "flying squad," a chariotry always ready for action on an instant's notice. Roads were always kept open for the wheeled vehicles of the flying squad. In the south were the estates and mansions of the vizier, the high priest, the commandant, the master of horse, sculptors' quarters, and not far from these were ateliers for glassmaking.

In the North City were large mansions and the North Palace, with beautiful wall paintings of bird life in the marshes; on the palace grounds were fishponds and aviaries and stables. Still farther to the north was a great double wall with a gate in it; on the wall over the gate was a room. We shall have occasion to mention it again.

During the decades since the first exploring expedition, more in the nature of an excursion, in the nineteenth century, from many countries have come archaeologists with spades, and work has been done, and still large parts of the city of Akhet-Aton remain for future excavators to explore. Since it was inhabited for only about fifteen years, archaeologists have not had the tedious and often difficult task, encountered in other places, of separating various levels of occupation. Heaps of imported ceramics were found in Akhet-Aton; these came from Mycenae on the Greek mainland, or at least they were of the same manufacture as those found in Mycenae. Archaeologists dubbed a street in Akhet-Aton "Greek Street" because of the abundance of this ware.[2] On the basis of it, the age of King Akhnaton is established as synchronous with the Mycenaean age in Greece, and the time of the Mycenaean age is fixed by the timetable of Egyptian chronology.

In this, his new capital, away from the stifling atmosphere of Thebes with its closed temples and discharged priesthood, Akhnaton enjoyed the life of a sovereign adored by his subjects, in the circle of his family, in lively intercourse with diplomats and ambassadors, attending temple services, traveling with his queen Nefretete in his royal vehicle of gold, and showering his favorites with royal gifts.

One of the most spectacular finds at Akhet-Aton was the famous painted head of Nefretete, a beautiful crowned head on a tall neck, today probably better known than any other sculptured head either of antiquity or of modern times. It was found by the German archaeological expedition, and long after her death Nefretete not only aroused admiration but was the cause of strife and accusations and strained international relations. According to the conditions of the license to dig, the first choice of objects found belonged to the Egyptian Department of Antiquities so that the National Museum in Cairo might be enriched. Only copies, molds, sherds, and other finds of lesser value could be kept by the finders and exported to their native countries; their profit was considered to be mainly scholarly— that of discovering, describing, and publishing. This prerogative the German expedition failed to exercise, and though more than four decades passed, with the exception of preliminary reports, no full account was submitted to the scientific world and the public in general. "Thanks to the fact that the Germans have only published their results in a most inadequate preliminary form, the objects which they found can only be

[2] H. Frankfort and J. D. S. Pendlebury, *The City of Akhenaten*, Part II (1933), p. 44.

regarded as so much loot from random excavations and the scientific knowledge acquired during the course of the work must be considered as lost."[3]

But the loot was worth while. All the finds were laid out on long tables, and the head of Nefretete was mingled with many molds and fragments of little value. The director of the Egyptian Department of Antiquities did not go over the material himself, for no important find had been announced; instead he sent a young assistant who passed the head as a piece to be released for removal from Egypt with the rest of the heap of broken pottery. Brought to Berlin, it was exhibited as a major piece of art and was photographed and reproduced in many periodicals. The ire of the Egyptian government was aroused. King Fuad himself requested and then demanded the return of the sculpture, but the Germans had no intention of doing so, and for many years diplomatic relations between the two countries were strained.

The head of Nefretete, which had survived so many vicissitudes, was also to witness and survive the Götterdämmerung. At the end of World War II the world of art breathed with relief when the radio announced that Nefretete had come through unscathed.

Sculpture was a great delight of the king of Akhet-Aton. Nowhere else have so many images in clay and in stone been found; Akhnaton was a great patron of this art. But for the most part it was he and the members of his family who were portrayed.

In the tombs destined for the aristocracy of Akhet-Aton, the figures of the pharaoh and his family regularly adorn the walls. The recipient of the tomb is also represented, a very small figure when compared with that of the king, receiving signs of

[3] Pendlebury, *Tell el-Amarna*, p. 168.

favor from the hands of the latter. Scenes of court life and of rural pursuits add to the pageantry.

On these bas-reliefs the king generally appears with his queen Nefretete, often accompanied by their daughters. Frequently Akhnaton is shown in attitudes of great affection toward his wife; and the bodies of the august pair are regularly presented covered only by thin tunics, with the breasts of the queen and her belly exposed for everyone to see. In this there is unmistakable exhibitionism, and in the king's exuberant pleasure in seeing himself portrayed thousands of times there is narcissism or self-adoration. (In this respect it is interesting that of Akhnaton and his immediate family we possess more original portraits in sculpture, low relief, and painting than of all the kings and queens of England together, from William the Conqueror to the present queen; many more were irretrievably lost through wanton destruction.) The peculiar features of Akhnaton—the very elongated head with deep-set eyes on a very thin and long neck, the flat chest, the hanging abdomen, thighs as thick as the swollen abdomen—were not minimized by the artists. On the contrary, they were stressed and made a mark of royal distinction. The royal servants on the bas-reliefs do not possess such crania, necks, abdomens, or thighs.

Often their daughters were pictured with the king and the queen. On some of the bas-reliefs in the tombs of Akhet-Aton two daughters of Akhnaton are shown, on others four, and in some cases six. The young princesses, still children, have the same extremely elongated heads on thin necks; and their heads, which for some reason have been shaved, reveal the peculiar shape with even greater clearness. In private scenes or in official receptions the king, his queen, and their daughters make a group that impresses the onlooker with the intimacy of their family life. The king rests his arm on the shoulders of his wife and touches her nipples with the tips of his fingers. This public display of affection is something entirely unfamiliar in the life of the pharaohs, as far as we can learn from Egyptian art. With the exception of Akhnaton, the pharaohs did not leave portraits of themselves in the nude.

The king loved his beautiful wife, was attached to his little daughters, was fond of sculpture and painting, was gifted with the talent of a poet, had a feeling of intimate contact with his deity, loved nature, and, judging from the pictures of musicians playing on their instruments, loved music too. The spades of the archaeologists turned up a capital built for the enjoyment of life.

In the year 1887 the state archive was discovered by chance by a fellah woman, who was digging next to her hut and found clay tablets covered with numerous signs. These were letters written in cuneiform, in Akkadian, the language of Assyro-Babylonia and of international diplomacy. I have quoted from some of the letters previously.[4] When some of the three hundred and sixty-odd tablets were first offered for sale, the authorities at both the Cairo Museum and at the Louvre pronounced them to be forgeries and worthless. Today they are priceless.

[4] The letters were published in a classical edition with a German translation by the Scandinavian scholar J. A. Knudtzon (1915); an English translation was made by S. A. B. Mercer, *The Tell el-Amarna Tablets* (1939). They are the subject of detailed discussion in *Ages in Chaos*, I, 223–335.

The Queen's Brother

Akhnaton did not wage wars and was rather indifferent to the raids made by various warring parties into his Asiatic domain. Letters from Syria and Palestine repeatedly called his attention to the danger of all his Asiatic provinces falling prey to the invaders, a bellicose king in the north and pillaging bands from the east. But Akhnaton was absorbed in his pleasures, in building his capital, in writing his poetry, and in his family life.

Scarcely a decade and a half later Akhet-Aton was left for desert sand to cover it. It was not until 1891–92 that, from under the hovels of the gypsy-like migratory settlement of the bedouin clan that bore the name of Amarna, the Petrie expedition slowly uncovered the city of Akhet-Aton. Of the palaces and houses nothing remained above the sand of the desert. One after another places of worship, palaces, sculptors' studios, and places of amusement came to light. The sepulchral chambers, however, had never been concealed from human eyes; these deserted rock chambers were known before the short-lived capital itself. They were built before the city proper was finished; it was more important for the Egyptian to have a house of eternity than a dwelling place; his entire philosophy of life was centered on the afterlife.

The tomb chambers of the nobles were carved in the face of

the surrounding rocky cliffs. There were two groups of them, one to the south, the other to the north. These sepulchers were generally modeled after the tombs of Thebes of the Eighteenth Dynasty. From a forecourt a door opens into a large hall, the roof of which is often supported by columns left in the solid rock when the tombs were cut out. Besides the hall there is a chamber with a statue of the owner of the sepulcher; this chamber is reached from the hall either directly or through an anteroom. The grave shaft is usually, though not always, in the front hall. The walls of the sepulcher are adorned with pictures in which body movements were caught with a realism unusual for the epoch of the New Kingdom. In these pictures lies the great interest that these tombs hold for Egyptologists and everyone interested in history and art.

The southern group of tombs is composed of the sepulchral apartments of Tutu, "The Chief Mouthpiece for the Foreign Countries";[1] Mahu, chief of gendarmery; Apy, royal scribe and steward; Nefer-Kheperu, governor of Akhet-Aton; May, royal chancellor and bearer of the fan of the king's right hand; Sutau, the overseer of the treasury; Suti, the standard-bearer; Any, scribe of the altar of Aton (a very old man, according to his picture); Paatenemheb, commander of the troops, and a few other equally important dignitaries.

All these were prominent members of the new aristocracy with important functions at court, in administration, in the army, or at the temple.

Among these tomb-gifts to the nobles, one was prepared for a man named Parennefer, who was of low origin and probably had little or no schooling; it was cut in the rock near the tomb of the high priest of Aton. According to the murals, he received other signs of royal benevolence. The wife of Parennefer is

[1] On his role in Syrian and Palestinian politics, see *Ages in Chaos*, I, 296–97.

shown meeting her happy husband after he had received royal gifts and honors.

H. Ranke, the eminent German Egyptologist, wondered at this distinction accorded Parennefer. "It appears that the favors are given to him because of some old relation to the king whom he served when the latter was an infant. He was apparently a simple servant," this servant "with clean hands"; he was made equal with the noblest of el-Amarna.[2]

This is the only extant reference to Akhnaton as an infant. It is unimportant except for the fact that Akhnaton, of whom nothing is known, not even by inference, until he occupied the throne, felt such deep gratitude to a servant who had performed some service long ago, in the king's very early childhood. Our thoughts turn to the servant who played a decisive role in saving the life of the infant Oedipus.

The Oedipus saga tells of a servant who carried the newborn prince to the wasteland with instructions to abandon him there; but the servant gave the child to a herdsman and his wife and they cared for the babe and later brought him to Corinth.

Was not the "simple servant" with "clean hands" who received high honors from the king for a service performed when the king was an infant the very man of whom the legend also preserved memory?

The southernmost rock tomb was built for Ay. Although it was left unfinished, it is immediately obvious that it was intended to be "the finest in the whole necropolis."[3] Three rows of four columns each were planned for either side of the central aisle of the first hall, but the work on the western side had scarcely begun. The walls were prepared to have pictures carved on them, but only one wall was carved, showing Ay and

[2] A. Erman–H. Ranke, *Aegypten und aegyptisches Leben im Altertum* (1923), pp. 133–34.

[3] Pendlebury, *Tell el-Amarna*, p. 54.

his wife, Ty, receiving gifts from Akhnaton and Nefretete. "It is significant of their intimacy with the royal family not only that Ty is there—the only instance of a woman being so honored—but also that the King and Queen as well as the princesses seem to be stark naked." In the next scenes the gifts Ay received are shown to marveling onlookers. Pendlebury described the pictures: "The doorkeepers of Ay's house hear the din and little urchins are sent to bring news. 'For whom is this rejoicing being made, my boy?' 'The rejoicing is being made for Ay the Divine Father, and Ty. They have been made people of gold!' A sentry says to a small boy, 'Hasten, go and see the loud rejoicing, I mean, who it is, and come back at a run!' The child darts out crying, 'I will do it. Look at me!' Another sentry has heard the news and tells his friend: '. . . Rise up and you will see this is a good thing which Pharaoh (Life! Prosperity! Health!) has done for Ay the Divine Father and Ty. Pharaoh (Life! Prosperity! Health!) has given them millions of loads of gold and all manner of riches!' "[4]

To his audience with the royal couple, Ay traveled in a triumphal procession, accompanied by a retinue of servants, a military guard of foreign troops, and ten scribes, the latter to write down all the events of the day.

There is no question that Ay was the most influential statesman in the days of Akhnaton. His power was even greater in the days of Tutankhamen, and after the premature death of the latter he became pharaoh of Egypt though he was not a prince by birth.

The titles Ay had when he served Akhnaton in Akhet-Aton (el-Amarna) were Father of the god, or Divine Father, Master of the Horse (or general of chariotry), "one trusted by the good god [the pharaoh] in the entire land," "foremost of the companions of the King," and several more. His wife, Ty, was named "the great nurse of the queen," meaning that she had

[4] Ibid., pp. 55–56.

brought up the queen. Many conjectures were offered as to the reason for Ay's spectacular rise, the significance of the title "Father of the god [king]," and the meaning of his wife's title. Did Ay advance because of his wife's position in the palace? But this position was not so exalted as to cause her husband to become, first, vizier, then regent, and finally king himself. Before Ay, the title "Father of the king" had been held by Yuya, father of Queen Tiy and father-in-law of Amenhotep III.

If we are on the right path in our search for the roots of the Oedipus legend in the closing years of the Eighteenth Dynasty, then clearly Ay was the prototype of Creon, who was influential in Thebes in the days following the death of Laius and the arrival of Oedipus. It was Creon who gave his sister, the queen, to Oedipus; it was he who had the most exalted position in the realm, second only to the king himself; it was he who coerced Oedipus into vacating the throne and who ruled the country in the days of the youthful Eteocles; and it was he who, after the premature death of the king, became king himself.

But this would also mean that Ay was a brother of Queen Tiy. I could not offer this solution and then use it solely to establish a needed parallel. It was therefore gratifying for me to see that this solution was arrived at, and only recently, by Cyril Aldred, who in 1957 published a paper in the *Journal of Egyptian Archaeology* on Ay's relationship to the royal house.[5] With very well chosen material he showed that Ay was a son of Yuya and Tuya and a brother of Queen Tiy. Ay also bore the same titles, designations, and appointments as Yuya—with the exception of the priestly office at the temple of the city of Ekhmim, an omission that is "explicable since Ay served Akhnaton and his god." But when Ay became king he showed a special interest in Ekhmim by building there a rock chapel to

[5] C. Aldred, "The End of the el-Amarna Period," *Journal of Egyptian Archaeology*, XLIII (1957), 30–41.

Min, "presumably because it was his birth-place, or the family seat, and he wished to honor his city god."

Ay, like Yuya—and the similarity of these pet names, used in their family, is also noteworthy—had a tomb prepared for himself in the days of Amenhotep III in the Valley of the Kings near Thebes, the tomb in which later Tutankhamen was placed, as Engelbach brought out, only a hundred and fifty yards from the tomb of Yuya. It is true that no inscription exists in which Ay says that he is a son of Yuya or a son of anybody, for that matter, and therefore Cyril Aldred wrote: "It is unfortunate that in the present state of our knowledge, the theory that Ay was a son, and probably the second son of Yuya, has to rest upon evidence that is no more than circumstantial; but if a relationship be accepted, with its corollary that Ay was a brother of Queen Tiy, it will explain much that is otherwise obscure in the history of the last years of the Eighteenth Dynasty. . . ."[6]

Aldred solved the problem correctly and it was modest of him to describe his evidence as circumstantial. The entire scene as we know it from the Greek cycle about the Theban royal house also points to Ay as the queen's own brother.

But Aldred solved one more problem, namely, that Ay was the father of Queen Nefretete. This was also assumed by earlier authors—for instance, Weigall[7] and Borchardt. Ay had the same title, "god's father," or "Divine Father," as Yuya before him, and this title, as Aldred conclusively brought out, signifies "father-in-law of the king."

[6] Ibid., p. 35.

[7] Weigall, *The Life and Times of Akhnaton*, p. 48.

The King's Mother and Wife

THE northernmost tomb in the northern group of sepulchers presented to royal favorites in their lifetime was excavated in the rock for Huya. Judged by the murals and inscriptions in the place prepared for his eternal rest, he must have been a very important official.[1] The murals also disclose that not everything was smooth and untroubled in Akhnaton's life.

In the twelfth year of his reign a drama that was long in the making became acute. The family life of the king, which seemed so idyllic, proved to be a tragedy. It is the pictures and inscriptions in Huya's sepulcher that make us aware of this.

The bas-reliefs in his tomb differ from those in other tombs in Akhet-Aton in that, besides King Akhnaton and his wife and children, the royal mother, Tiy, is repeatedly represented; actually she appears to play a dominant role. No other tomb in Akhet-Aton that has been opened reveals so much of the life of the royal family as the tomb of Huya. He was "the Superintendent of the House, of the Double Treasury, and of the Harem of the Great Royal Wife, Tiy." These, his three functions, are repeated many times in the texts on the walls of his sepulchral chambers. More often, in Huya's enumeration of offices it is said: ". . . and of the Harem of the King's Mother and Great Royal Wife, Tiy." He was in the service of Tiy.

The appellation "King's Mother and Great Royal Wife"

[1] Davies, *The Rock Tombs of el-Amarna*, III (1905).

applied to the dowager queen is usually interpreted to mean that she was queen mother to the reigning monarch and royal wife to the deceased pharaoh, but this explanation does not completely clear up the peculiarity of Tiy's title.

Huya's tomb was built in the twelfth year of Akhnaton's reign; the text to some of the bas-reliefs begins with "Year 12" (for instance, "Year 12, the second month of winter, the eighth day"). Amenhotep III, Akhnaton's father, had been dead for almost twelve years. For as many years after his death his widow had kept a harem for the dead monarch. This is difficult to understand.

Huya, according to his pictures and inscriptions, was appointed to his offices under Akhnaton. Why should the king have appointed Huya to the office of "superintendent of the harem" of Tiy, royal mother, dowager queen?

The harem of the queen mother and royal wife, Tiy, was in Akhet-Aton, the capital founded four years after Amenhotep III passed away.

According to oriental custom, the chief wife of the king, his queen, kept a harem for her husband. This absence of jealousy on the part of the queen, who supplied the king with concubines, was natural in the Orient. We met this custom in the house of the young patriarch Jacob, whose wives Leah and Rachel competed with each other and used to send their husband to their handmaids, their reciprocal jealousy being expressed in the number of progeny a wife and her handmaid could produce, in an effort to exceed the fruitfulness of the rival wife and her handmaid. In the royal harem of Egypt insensibility to what a modern Western woman would regard as her sacred rights was displayed, though not for the purpose of an increased harvest of children. The puzzling thing is not that Tiy kept a harem for her husband but that she kept it for twelve years after she became a widow, that it was built in the new capital, which her husband did not live by several years to see, and that King Akhnaton, Tiy's son, who built her harem, also appointed a superintendent for this new establishment.

The dowager queen's beauty is praised in the inscriptions of Huya's tomb: "Praise to thy Ka [soul], O Lady of the Two Lands who makes the Two Lands light with her beauty, the Queen Mother and Great Queen Tiy." She is blessed "with pleasure and delight every day."

Among the bas-reliefs in Huya's tomb are two depicting a royal family banquet: on both of them Akhnaton sits facing Tiy; behind him sits Nefretete. It could have been an entertainment; it could also have been a scene of some deliberation or negotiations accompanied by food and drink. On one of these murals, "while Akhnaton attacks with his hands a broiled bone as long as his arm, Nefretete makes as direct an onslaught on a fair-sized bird." Akhnaton and Nefretete wear simple headdresses, whereas Tiy is crowned with the double plumes and the horned disk. Tiy has food before her but does not eat. Two little princesses sit next to Nefretete; one little princess sits next to Tiy. This last little princess, Beketaten, was for a long time thought to have been the youngest of the children of Akhnaton and Nefretete.

The eldest daughter of the royal pair was Meritaten, who later reigned as Smenkhkare's queen; on the bas-relief of the banquet she is a child of six or seven years. The second daughter was Meketaten, who died young. When she died the royal parents grieved, and the royal artist pictured them on the walls of her sepulchral chamber sorrowful in their bereavement. The third daughter was Ankhesenpaaten, who later reigned as Tutankhamen's queen. The fourth and sometimes also the fifth and sixth daughters are portrayed on the bas-reliefs in various sepulchral chambers of Akhet-Aton and in a family group that was found in the ruins of the palace in that capital. Only in the sepulcher of Huya is little Beketaten pictured, in the banquet scenes and in certain others. From these scenes it has been concluded that the youngest daughter of Akhnaton was his favorite child.

Flinders Petrie, the Egyptologist, wrote: "The princess Beketaten has been usually placed as a seventh and youngest daughter of Akhnaton. She occurs, however, in a tomb of his twelfth year, or only six years after the second daughter was born; and she appears among the daughters where four or six are shown, hence the difficulty as to her position. . . ." Petrie solved the problem by demonstrating that Beketaten was not the youngest daughter of Nefretete but a daughter of Tiy. She is "always associated with Tyi [Tiy], she sits by the side of Tyi, while the daughters of Akhenaten [Akhnaton] sit by their mother; she alone follows Tyi in a procession where no other children appear. Moreover, she is never called other than a King's Daughter whereas all the other princesses in every inscription are entitled Daughters of Nefretete. Thus, by the difficulty about her position in the family, by her constant association with Tyi, and her being differently titled than the others, it seems clear that she was the youngest and favorite child of Tyi."[2]

Beketaten was considered to be a younger daughter of Akhnaton and Nefretete because her picture and name appear in bas-relief and inscriptions for the first time in the twelfth year of Akhnaton's reign; her body is smaller than that of Ankhesepaaten, the third daughter of the royal couple in one of the banquet scenes of that year; she is also smaller than the four little princesses in the lintel scene, the story of which follows shortly; the divine part of her name (Aten) is in the names of Akhnaton's daughters, as well as in his own.

N. de Garis Davies, in his description of the necropolis of Akhet-Aton, agreed with Petrie, and all the other scholars followed suit: Beketaten was not a daughter of Nefretete; she was

2 W. M. Flinders Petrie, A History of Egypt (7th ed.; 1924), II, 204.

a daughter of Tiy, and consequently it was concluded that her father was the late Amenhotep III and not his son, Akhnaton.

On the second mural bearing a scene of a banquet, Tiy is once more entertained by Akhnaton and Nefretete; all of them have cups out of which they drink wine or some other beverage. Beketaten stands next to the chair of her mother, Tiy; two little princesses, Meketaten and Ankhesenpaaten, stand next to their mother, Nefretete. Once more it is Queen Tiy who wears the double plumes of the empire; Akhnaton and Nefretete have, as in other pictures, only the royal emblem of the cobra on their foreheads. The subject of the conversation going on between Akhnaton, Nefretete and Tiy is not recorded. In the light of later developments the impression is that some family affair is being discussed in all earnestness.

For the third time the little princess Beketaten is shown, or, more correctly, her image is shown being prepared by Auta, "the overseer of sculptors" (literally "vivifiers") of the great royal wife Tiy. Auta sits on a low stool before the statue of Beketaten and puts the final touches of paint on the likeness, working with devotion, even affection. From the proportions of her body, Beketaten appears to be a young child.

In the twelfth year of Akhnaton's reign Beketaten was a small child, four, five, or at the most six years old. Amenhotep III had been dead for about twelve years; no wonder the little girl was thought to be a daughter of Akhnaton and Nefretete. However, when it was determined that she was not a daughter of Nefretete, but of Tiy, it was concluded that she was the child of Amenhotep III, Tiy's husband.

N. de G. Davies thought he found support for this position. On the lintel of the doorway leading to the inner rooms of Huya's tomb there is a bas-relief with two scenes, one on the right, the other on the left. Davies wrote: "I was much inclined, like my predecessors, to give them no further attention." The left-hand scene shows Akhnaton sitting with Nefretete. He has his right arm on her shoulder; she rests her left arm on his

AKHNATON WITH THE REGALIA. *(Cairo Museum)*

AKHNATON WITH WIFE AND DAUGHTER WORSHIPING ATON. *(el Amarna)*

QUEEN NEFRETETE. PAINTED LIMESTONE. *(Wiesbaden)*

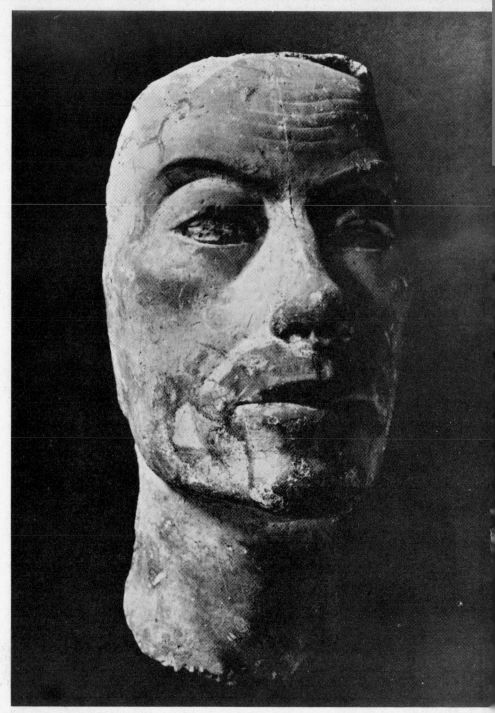

AY, QUEEN TIY'S BROTHER AND FUTURE KING. A MASK. *(Berlin Museum)*

AKHNATON IN LATER YEARS. *(Cairo Museum)*

LINTEL IN HUYA'S TOMB: LEFT SIDE. *(el Amarna)*

BANQUET SCENE. *(Huya's Tomb)*

LINTEL IN HUYA'S TOMB: RIGHT SIDE

BANQUET SCENE. (*Huya's Tomb*)

AKHNATON LEADING TIY AND BEKETATEN TO THE TEMPLE. *(Huya's Tomb)*

knee and turns her face to his. Four daughters in front of them wave fans for their parents. The right-hand scene shows the king sitting with his face toward Queen Tiy. In front of Tiy, with one arm on the queen's knee and the other arm lifted toward the king, is Beketaten. Three female attendants are added to balance the opposite picture in which four little princesses are depicted. The royal figures are naked.

Tiy is described: "The hereditary princess, great of favor, lady of grace, charming in loving-kindness, filling the palace with her beauty, Mistress of South and North, the great wife of the king, whom he loves, the lady of the Two Lands, Tiy."

Next to Beketaten is written: "The king's daughter of his body, beloved by him, Beketaten."

On the basis of these statements accompanying the bas-reliefs, Davies in his publication about the tomb expressed the opinion that the right portion of the lintel relief depicts not Akhnaton but his father, Amenhotep III.[3] In other words, that

[3] An inscription on the right jamb under the lintel lists the names of the King of South and North who liveth in truth, Lord of the Two Lands, Nefer-Kheperu-re Ua-en-re, who gives life, Lord of the Two Lands, Nebmaatre, and of the Great King's Wife and King's Mother, Tiy, who lives forever and ever.

Nefer-Kheperu-re Ua-en-re are names of Akhnaton, known from different sources; also in the el-Amarna letters Akhnaton is regularly called by the name of Naphuria, which is an intimate rendering of Nefer-Kheperu-re. Davies suggested that Nebmaatre means a separate person, namely King Amenhotep III. He admitted, however: "It must be noticed that as the King [Akhnaton] became more and more sensitive to any mention of discarded deities, the figures of the goddesses Maat and Mut were abandoned even in spelling, and hence the prenomen of Amenhotep is given in an unusual form, while his personal name could not be cited at all."

Mutilating his father's name on inscriptions, Akhnaton used to replace the name Amenhotep with his prenomen Nebmaatre, and the full name then read Nebmaatre-Nebmaatre, in both instances the word Maat (Truth) being not spelled but shown as the goddess' figure. In the case before us it is spelled out. On the inscriptions accompanying the picture on the right side of the lintel, "Living in Truth" (ankh-em-Maat) immediately precedes the prenomen Nebmaatre, and this appellative Akhnaton used only in reference to himself. Also "Living in Truth" precedes the name Nebmaatre on the canopy of Tiy described later in this book.

the lintel shows on the left side Akhnaton and his wife and children, and on the right his father, Amenhotep III, his mother, Tiy, and his little sister, Beketaten.

Davies recognized that in his interpretation lay "a difficulty of reconciling the situation with other records." The king had been dead for more than a decade, yet on these murals the daughter, whom Davies, in order to resolve chronological difficulties, described as born to him posthumously, was the same size and age as on bas-reliefs in the same tomb dated the twelfth year of Akhnaton's reign. This was but one of the difficulties. Davies tried to overcome them by explaining: The two family scenes on the lintel signified "in what full sympathy the conforming king and his nonconforming son were," a sympathy that "must have been based on the essential unity of thought and policy." This surmise is very farfetched. The king, who never called himself "son of Amenhotep" or "son of Neb-maat-ra," who, further, erased the name of his father Amenhotep, wherever he found it, could scarcely be said to have been in "sympathy" or in "unity of thought" with him.

Were the two lintel scenes an echo of an earlier co-regency? This cannot be either, because there had been no co-regency between the father and the son who mounted the throne in complete ignorance of the affairs of the state in previous years, and was advised in a letter from a foreign king to find out from his mother about the relations between their states in the time of his father; and the very fact that the son mutilated the name of Amenhotep III on all monuments and inscriptions prior to his move to el-Amarna makes the hypothesis of a co-regency seem untenable.

There remained only a hypothesis of a metaphysical character: "Amenhotep was dead; but so long as his capable queen survived, his reign could scarcely be said to be ended and it may only be in a technical sense that we have to deny a co-regency [between father and son] at this period after all."[4]

A co-regency after the death of a king between the living and the dead?

The main reason for identifying the king in the right-hand picture on the lintel as Amenhotep III is the presence of Beketaten, she being a daughter of Tiy and referred to as "the king's daughter of his body." But Beketaten's presence in this picture is precisely an argument to compromise this identification of the king as Amenhotep III. She is here presented as she was in the twelfth year of Akhnaton, a little girl, smaller than the four daughters of Nefretete, at that time not yet seven years old. Even if Akhnaton could, in a symbolic sense, have co-ruled with his father after the latter's death, which is very questionable, his father could not have begotten a child five years after his death, which is not questionable.

The king in the right-hand picture on the lintel is not presented as one who is dead being worshiped by the living: a ray of Aton holds a sign of *life* at his mouth, and another ray from the solar disk holds a similar sign close to the mouth of Tiy.

Pendlebury also noticed this, though he failed to draw any conclusions from it: "There is no distinction between the two groups, that is to say it is not a case of the living on one side and the dead on the other."[5]

The very fact that the king is pictured under the disk of Aton is a strong indication that he is Akhnaton. Furthermore, the build of the body of the king, shown nude with a hanging abdomen, is that of Akhnaton, not Amenhotep III. The headdress, which is round in form, differs from the headdress of the king in the left-hand picture on the lintel yet is identical with the headdress of Akhnaton in the two pictures of the banquet in the same sepulcher. The king was a living one and his pose,

[4] Davies, *The Rock Tombs of el-Amarna*, III, 16.

[5] *Journal of Egyptian Archaeology*, XXII (1936), 198.

with one arm half raised and the other resting on a knee, is almost the same as in the picture of the banquet. Queen Tiy also has a very similar pose in both likenesses, at the meal and on the lintel, with one arm raised and the other hanging at her side. And in both likenesses, in the banquet scene and on the lintel, Akhnaton and Tiy sit opposite each other.[6]

Finally, the very inscription accompanying Queen Tiy on the right-hand side of the lintel, which suggests that she sits opposite her husband, could scarcely refer to a deceased husband. I repeat the passage, this time in Maspero's translation:

"The hereditary princess the most praised, the lady of grace, sweet in her love, who fills the palace with her beauties, the regent, the Mistress of South and North, the great wife of the king who loves him, the Lady of both lands, Teye [Tiy]."

Maspero expressed his astonishment at this description of Queen Tiy: "Exactly as if her husband were still living."[7]

It is unusual and certainly improper to say of a widowed queen in an inscription, "sweet in her love" or "who fills the palace with her beauties." Neither the name of the king, nor the fact that he is pictured on the lintel with a sign of life before him, nor the physique of the king lend the slightest credibility to the conjecture that the figure in question represents Amenhotep III. The fact that Aton is pictured, that the name of the little daughter also contains the divine part, Aton, and that the widowed queen is spoken of as a sweetheart of the king, all are evidence against this hypothesis. The known animosity of Akhnaton toward the memory of his father is still another point against the hypothesis. Finally, the age of

[6] This disposes of Cyril Aldred's conjecture that because on one side of the lintel the king sits with his queen and on the other opposite the queen, thus disturbing a symmetry in the position of the members of two households, Amenhotep must have been dead; he did not question the identity of the king opposite Tiy on the lintel.

[7] G. Maspero in Theodore M. Davis, *The Tomb of Queen Tiyi* (1910), p. xx.

Beketaten, who was born six to eight years after Amenhotep's death, leaves no room for the assumption that the figure on the right-hand portion of the lintel is Amenhotep III; the king, the father of Beketaten ("the king's daughter of his body"), is Akhnaton.

Should the reader still harbor some doubt as to the correctness of this interpretation, another picture from the same tomb may dispel such skepticism. On this bas-relief, on the east wall of the sepulchral chamber, King Akhnaton leads Queen Tiy into the temple; they are followed by the princess Beketaten. "Akhenaten is leading Tyi [Tiy] affectionately by the hand, and his little sister Beketaten follows with a gift for the altar on behalf of each."[8] Two nurses watch over the child, and there is the usual retinue of attendants and officials.

Actually this is the very same combination of participants as on the right side of the lintel: Akhnaton, Tiy, and Beketaten. In front of the king is written: "Conducting the great Queen and Queen Mother, Tiy, to let her see her Sun-shade."[9] The sun-shade was a division of a temple. In the sanctuary of Aton in Akhet-Aton there was a shade for Akhnaton, another for Tiy, and still another for the little Beketaten.

Akhnaton wears a transparent tunic that allows his body to be seen: his scrawny neck, protruding stomach, and swollen upper legs. Tiy is almost nude; she has a crown of plumes and the horned disk on her head; the outlines of her breasts, abdomen, and legs are clearly visible. Akhnaton holds Tiy's hand. They advance toward the inner portal of the temple as lovers, not as a son and a mother.

"My wife who is my mother," says Oedipus of Jocasta. "My daughter who is my sister," he says of Antigone.

[8] Davies, *The Rock Tombs of el-Amarna*, III, 8.

[9] Ibid., p. 7.

Incest

INCEST between brother and sister was a very usual, even quite regular, affair in the palace of Egypt. The throne under the Eighteenth Dynasty was inherited in theory, or allegory, not by a son but by a daughter, and the son, by marrying the heiress, his sister or half sister, acquired title to the throne. Even if this procedure did not take place in all cases, it was thought a desirable prerequisite in the royal succession of a father by his son. This system of succession assured the royal house of perpetuation. The incestuous feature was not considered immoral; moral values, especially in the sexual life of races, clans, and classes, are to a great extent dependent on local habits, beliefs, superstitions, and traditions. In the Egyptian language the word "sister" is often substituted for the word "wife": in poems and songs sweethearts call each other "brother" and "sister." Incest between mother and son, however, was an abominable thing in the eyes of the Egyptians. The ancient world, primitive society, the modern world, all equally abhorred and abhor "the wretched mother's slumber at the side of her own son."[1] In the scale of relationships a mother is a first-degree relative, a sister a second-degree relative. Issue produced by one's own mother is the most bastardly. The procreating scheme of nature is disturbed, and a deep-seated protest against the

[1] Sophocles, *Antigone*, ll. 862–63.

96

deep-rooted urge manifests itself in laws and usages of civilized and uncivilized peoples alike.

The motif of a brother and sister being separated in childhood, meeting and falling in love, marrying, and discovering to their horror that their marriage is incestuous, is one that has been used and abused in folk tales, legends, and modern novels. Occasionally, too, a story of such a drama gets into the newspapers.

The incestuous urge between mother and son may be strong but it is usually unconscious and often takes the reverse form of rejection of the mother by the son. In a very few cases incest does take place between mother and son; perhaps the most famous instance was that of Nero and Agrippina, to which the emperor himself hinted and Suetonius attested, but which may have taken place only in Nero's fantasy, as other historians (Tacitus) assumed. As an actor, Nero loved to play the part of Oedipus. But a story in which a son takes his mother to wife without knowing of their blood relationship must not be accepted credulously. So in the case of Akhnaton, the drama was not that a son married his mother in ignorance of their blood ties but that he knowingly made his mother his consort not only on the throne but also in bed, as well as fathering a child by her.

If there was secrecy about the relations between mother and son at first there was no such secrecy later. It must have been part of the tradition that grew into a legend about the tragic fate of Akhnaton and his house that relations between the king and his mother were kept secret for only a short time. Homer says that the union of son and mother was "speedily made known."

King Burraburias, the only monarch of the period who dared to speak to the pharaoh as a superior to an inferior, and whose historical identity was clarified in *Ages in Chaos*, wrote in a letter to Akhnaton: "For the mistress of thy house I have sent only twenty seal rings of beautiful lapis lazuli because she had not done anything for me that I had requested, she did not lift up my head when I was sorrowful." At the same time the king from the north demanded presents which he enumerated in a long list.

The mistress mentioned in the letter was Tiy. "The mistress here referred to has been taken to have been Tiy, the queen mother who, in this case, which is an exception to the general rule in Egypt, played a great role."[2] The words "the mistress of thy house," addressed to Akhnaton and meaning his mother, Tiy, signify that knowledge of the new relationship had reached the palaces of foreign countries.

There were family ties between the house of Amenhotep III and the house of the kings of Mitanni, to which the el-Amarna tablets bear witness. Amenhotep's mother, the wife of Thutmose IV, was a Mitannian princess, Mutemwija. In the tenth year of Amenhotep III's reign a Mitannian princess by the name of Gilukhipa was dispatched to Thebes with a retinue and a rich dowry to become one of the secondary wives of the pharaoh. It has also been repeatedly conjectured that one of Tiy's parents was of Mitannian origin. Before the end of Amenhotep's reign the king of Mitanni sent another princess, named Tadukhipa, to the pharaoh, but when she arrived the king was no longer alive; she was at the disposal of Amenhotep IV, who became Akhnaton after he mounted the throne.

The close family relations of these two houses make it very probable that Akhnaton, when sent away in childhood to comply with the oracular ban or, more probably, to circumvent the dire prophecy, was dispatched to Mitanni, to the relatives of Amenhotep and Tiy.

The whereabouts of the kingdom of Mitanni is not positively known. In view of the close contact between the Mitannian and

[2] Mercer, *The Tell el-Amarna Tablets,* note to Letter 11; see also J. A. Knudtzon, *Die El-Amarna Tafeln* (1915), p. 1031.

Egyptian royal houses, modern historians usually place Mitanni in northern Syria, in the neighborhood of Carchemish on the Euphrates, though this region, as is well known, was in the domain of Assyria, where Arameans, "Hurrians," and "Hittites" occupied parts of the crowded territory. There is reason to believe that this geographical assignment is incorrect and that Mitanni was in northern Iran, where Herodotus in the fifth century before the present era described the people of Matiene: this Persian satrapy was near Mount Ararat.[3]

Though the geographical position of Mitanni may be a matter of controversy, the religious affiliation of its people is known for certain. The kings of that people prayed to and swore by Mitra, Varuna, Indra, and other Indo-Iranian gods. And this point is important to the matter that I should like to elucidate. The Iranians (Persians) had an approach to the problem of incest very different from that of other peoples of antiquity. They had an ethical religious concept and practice of *xvaetva-datha* or *xvetokdas*, which means, according to ancient authors and modern scholars alike, the marriage of parents with their children and of uterine brothers and sisters. The ancient Iranian texts commend and even command *xvaetvadatha;* in certain religious ceremonies only a young man who has undertaken it may officiate. "Corpse-bearers may be purified, not only with the urine of cattle [sacred cow[4]], but also with the mingled urine of a man and a woman who have performed *xvaetva-datha*."[5] Obviously it was not only the royal house that practiced incest but the Persians of various ranks too.[6] Marital re-

[3] Herodotus, v. 49. On this subject I shall have more to say in a sequel to *Ages in Chaos.*

[4] Cf. *Worlds in Collision*, "Cow-worship."

[5] Article, "Marriage" (Iranian), in Vol. VIII of the *Encyclopedia of Religion and Ethics*, ed. J. Hastings.

[6] Quintus Curtius Rufus (viii. ii. 19) tells of the Bactrian satrap Sisimithres who married his mother.

lations with mother, daughter, and sister among the Persians
are reported with odium by Diogenes Laertius, Strabo, Plutarch,
and among the Fathers of the Church by Clement of Alexandria
and Hieronymus (St. Jerome). Philo of Alexandria wrote that
children from the union of a mother and son were deemed by
the Iranians to be particularly well born; and Catullus stated
that a magus (a Mazda priest) is the fruit of incestuous relations between mother and son,[7] and Strabo declared such
marriages to have been an ancient custom among the Persians.[8]
"These Magi, by ancestral custom, consort even with their
mothers. Such are the customs of the Persians."

The Greek and Latin authors named here all belonged to the
last century before the present era or to the earlier centuries
of this era. They wrote of sexual relations between a son and
mother as arousing horror; these practices must have appeared
no less unnatural to the Greeks of earlier centuries.

The classical authors did not err in telling of incestuous marriages among the Indo-Iranians, or Persians. In the Pahlavi religious and juridical texts references to xvaetvadatha, there
called xvetokdas, are numerous. "Observance of it is one of the
surest signs of piety in the coming days of evil . . . it expiates
mortal sin and forms the one insuperable barrier to the attacks
of Aeshm, the incarnation of Fury (Sayast la-Sayast, VIII. 18;
XVIII, 3 f.); it is especially obnoxious to demons, whose power
it impairs (Dinkart, III. 82); it is the second of the seven good
works of religion, its neglect the fourth of the thirty heinous
sins, and it is the ninth of the thirty-three ways of gaining
heaven. It is even said to have been prescribed by Zarathustra
as the eighth of his ten admonitions to mankind (Dinkart, III.
195)."[9] This religious book of Dinkart also tells of a controversy

[7] Catullus, xc. 3.

[8] Strabo, xv. 3. 20.

[9] From the article, "Marriage" (Iranian), in Vol. VIII of the Encyclopedia of Religion and Ethics, ed. J. Hastings.

on this subject between a Zoroastrian theologian and a Jewish objector, the former declaring: "That union [between] father and daughter, son and her who bore him, and brother and sister, is the most complete that I have considered."[10]

The kings of Mitanni, being worshipers of the Indo-Iranian gods, must have regarded incest between mother and son as not only a pardonable relation but a holy union. These kings were on the most intimate terms with Amenhotep III, Tiy, and Akhnaton, because of the family relationships. I have conjectured that Akhnaton, who spent his childhood and youth away from the paternal home, probably grew up in the palace of his Mitannian relatives—the sending of a Mitannian lass to the Theban palace is documented by the letters of el-Amarna—and it may well have been the influence of the customs of Mitanni that led Akhnaton and Tiy to enter into marital relations.

E. A. Wallis Budge, a learned Egyptologist of the earlier part of this century, compared the language of Akhnaton's hymns to that of the Vedas and traced the origin of the idea of picturing the sun with rays ending in hands to the long golden arms of the Vedic sun god Surya.[11] H. R. Hall added: "We remember that Mitanni had an Indo-Iranian element in its population which venerated the Indian gods Mitra, Varuna, Indra." In "handed rays" traceable to Mitanni we have another proof that Mitannian or Indo-Iranian concepts made their way into the palace of Thebes. The sacredness of incestuous relations was one of these concepts.

After his complete rupture with the priests of Amon, Akhnaton apparently did not wish to keep his relation to his mother a secret. He boasted of "living in truth," and this phrase is an appellation attached to his proper name. After a period of indecision and concealment he made up his mind to bring his

[10] Trans. E. W. West, pp. 399ff.

[11] E. A. Wallis Budge, *Tutankhamen, Amenism, Atenism and Egyptian Monotheism* (1923).

relation into the open and to compel the Egyptians to regard this union as holy and admirable. Thus he openly led his mother-wife and their daughter to their shades in the temple of Akhet-Aton, had this procession cut in wall bas-reliefs, and had it written of Beketaten, their child, that she was "the king's daughter of his body."

However, this innovation in religion and morals—incest between son and mother—was alien to the Egyptians, whose gods, religious customs, and ethics even then went back to gray antiquity; and when under Akhnaton it came into the open, the eruption of discontent was not long in coming.

Nefretete

IN THE same mural that shows Akhnaton tenderly leading his mother-wife to the shrine, followed by Beketaten, Huya, the owner of the tomb, is depicted in a lower row, leading officials and servants, and the inscription reads: "The appointment of the superintendent of the royal harem [of Queen Tiy], Huya." Queen Tiy is referred to in these words: "She who rises in beauty."

It is generally assumed that Tiy remained in Thebes for several years after Akhnaton moved to Akhet-Aton.[1] "Apparently Tiy had come to settle in Akhet-Aton. A house had been provided for her, a shrine erected for her worship, and the personnel of her household chosen."

A "House of Tiy" was also mentioned on a sherd from Akhet-Aton described by Petrie.[2] Whether she moved early to Akhet-Aton or came later, in the twelfth year of Akhnaton's reign the drama of his family life ripened. He had two households, and these are pictured on the bas-reliefs of the banquet and on the lintel. The king's mother-wife claimed official status and a privileged position for herself and her child. Tiy was not a weakling, and one of the two women soon had to go, either Tiy or Nefretete.

[1] Borchardt regards Medinet el-Ghurab near Fayum as the residence of the dowager queen.

[2] Petrie, *Tell el-Amarna*, p. 33.

For the last five years of Akhnaton's reign there is no mention of Queen Nefretete. "History does not tell us what was the final fate of Nefertiti [Nefretete]. . . . Her end, it would seem, must have been very sorrowful," writes Arthur Weigall in *The Life and Times of Akhnaton*.[3]

The discussions that took place between Akhnaton and Nefretete on one side and Tiy on the other give the impression that Akhnaton was at first loyal to his queen, who, as though shielded by him, sat behind him. Tiy, however, insisted on the status of chief (great) queen for herself, and during the negotiations wore the double plumes and the horned disk on her head. There could be but one great queen, and if Tiy's claim were upheld Nefretete would be reduced to the role of one among many royal wives, actually a concubine, and her children to the corresponding status of harem children. It appears that Akhnaton, under attack by Tiy, tried to preserve two households, as the scenes on the lintel suggest. But in the triumphant scene of Tiy going with Akhnaton and Beketaten to the temple of Akhet-Aton, where three shrines were prepared, one for the king, one for Tiy, and one for their daughter, but none for Nefretete and her children, Tiy apparently has achieved complete victory. Her son has recognized her as his official wife and the child as his royal daughter. Nefretete, "the beautiful has come," who had shared with her husband all the glamor of past years, could not accept her new position as a concubine, while her husband made his mother-wife the chief consort.

"Shortly after this twelfth year came the heaviest blow of all. His wife, Nefretete, unless we have misinterpreted the evidence, deserted him," wrote Professor T. E. Peet, in his "Akhenaten, Ty, Nefertete and Mutnezemt."[4] But he did not know the cause of this desertion: "Had the contemplative life begun to pall on her? or the adherents of Amun in Thebes seen

[3] P. 233.

[4] In Brunton, *Kings and Queens of Ancient Egypt*, p. 113.

in her a popular rival to her husband for the throne? We do not know and we may never know."

Still another historian, S. R. K. Glanville ("Amenophis III and His Successors in the XVIII Dynasty"[5]), wrote: "With regard to Nefertiti's disappearance, it is generally agreed" that it was the result "of her disgrace some time after the year 12." Her name was erased from certain monuments, the name of Akhnaton on them being left intact.

Professor H. Frankfort "made a strong case for thinking that the great changes took place in year 12 through the arrival of Tiy. . . . Frankfort suggested that Tiy's arrival and the great honor paid to her is connected in some way with the disappearance of Nefertiti."[6] Frankfort recognized the fact of the struggle between the two queens but he thought the rivalry was purely for political power. The true meaning of the contest was dynastic and conjugal.

J. D. S. Pendlebury, however, thought that Nefretete moved away from Akhnaton and his royal house to a residence north of the city, on its outskirts, where the cliffs approach the Nile. Behind a double wall was a structure, "only a little of [which] remains, but enough objects were found to suggest that it belonged to Nefertiti and, since the paintings from the gateway in the wall show that the wall can be assigned to a date after the Queen's fall from power, it is a reasonable assumption that it was to this palace that she retired."[7] In her vexation over the turn in her life, or in her unhappiness at anticipating the rift to come, her beautiful face became sorrowful—"everyone knows the famous head of Nefertiti in Berlin; not so many have seen the even more charming statuette of her when she was getting older and sad and disillusioned."[8]

[5] In Brunton, *Great Ones of Ancient Egypt* (1930), p. 131.

[6] Ibid., pp. 131–32.

[7] *Tell el-Amarna*, p. 45.

[8] Ibid., p. 135.

Two parties are often spoken of as continuing to struggle for power, that of Akhnaton and Tiy and that of the banned Nefretete. Ay was on Nefretete's side: he was her father and he led her camp against his sister and son-in-law.

In a variant of the Greek legend Oedipus sends his younger wife Euryganeia, mother of four of his children, away in disgrace.[9] It appears that the story of Nefretete's disgrace served as a motif for that tradition, known in antiquity though not exploited by the tragedians of the fifth century.

The drama at Akhet-Aton did not come to an end with the disappearance or disgrace of Nefretete, and could scarcely be expected to have done so. The gallery of pictures in the tombs, in the ateliers of the artists, in the ruins of the palaces cease to relate what was taking place in Akhet-Aton. For four or five years after the desertion or disgrace of Nefretete Akhnaton continued to occupy the throne. It is generally agreed that some tragedy occurred in the personal life of the king. It is also agreed that Ay became even more powerful and was directing the fortunes of the state and the palace. And, finally, it is agreed that after a while Tiy was no longer present. Her end is shrouded in mystery because she was not buried like a great queen of a great empire; on pages to come we shall follow her funeral cortege to a hiding place where her catafalque was left broken, its sides scattered.

The ultimate fate of Nefretete is not known. She followed the guidance of her father, Ay, in her stand against Akhnaton. Pendlebury, in his popular book *Tell el-Amarna*, tells a story that he would not repeat in his scientific report of the excavations, *The City of Akhnaton*. This is what he says: "No objects which must have come from her burial were found in the royal tomb. The only clue we have is that in the 'eighties of the last century a body of men was seen marching down the high desert

[9] Bethe, *Thebanische Heldenlieder*, pp. 26, 141.

with a golden coffin, and shortly afterwards appeared golden objects bearing her name, whether genuine or faked it is hard to say. That is a well-known story and is told of almost every site in Egypt."[10]

I do not speak as a scholar when I express this thought, but perhaps it is better that only sculptures and no mummy of Nefretete remain. Her sculptured head is regarded as the embodiment of dazzling beauty, insensitive to the passage of time, unspoiled by centuries that have witnessed the decay of empires. Nefretete has emerged from the ruins of the ancient capital on the Nile as a symbol of imperishable beauty. It is sad to see in her last portrait how tired and sorrowful she grew; but it would be an unpleasant reminder of how perishable is our clay if a grinning face of the mummified queen could look at us from a page opposite the portrait of her who bore in life the appellation, "Beauty forever and ever."

[10] Pendlebury, *Tell el-Amarna*, pp. 169–70. Cf. *Journal of Egyptian Archaeology*, IV (1917), 45.

The King Deposed

BEFORE his reign was over Akhnaton was keeping the prince Smenkhkare—a youth in his teens—close to himself and for a year or so even made him a co-ruler. There is preserved a sculpture of Akhnaton kissing Smenkhkare, a young boy sitting on his lap. For a while after it was found this sculpture was thought to represent Akhnaton caressing Nefretete. But then it was recognized that the figure on his lap is the likeness of Smenkhkare. There is also a bas-relief in which Akhnaton sits next to Smenkhkare, already a youth, at a dining table, one arm resting on Smenkhkare's shoulder, the fingers of the other hand touching his chin. The erotic atmosphere of this bas-relief has led some scholars to express the opinion that Akhnaton was stirred by unnatural desires.

"The co-regency between Akhnaton and Smenkhkare has always been assumed, but here are signs of a more intimate relationship. A stela in [the] Berlin [Museum], until recently supposed to represent Akhnaton and Nefretete, has now been recognized as an instance of the king's expression of feeling for his young co-regent."[1]

As we shall see in the pages to follow, in the opinion of the anatomist who studied the mummies of Smenkhkare and

[1] Glanville, in Brunton, *Great Ones of Ancient Egypt*, p. 129. Professor Newberry expressed himself in a more definite way on the subject.

Tutankhamen, both were sons of Akhnaton, and this view is now accepted as the one that is most highly probable. If so, Akhnaton's display of affection toward his elder son may be understood as an expression of paternal feeling. However, with the king "living in truth" it is hard to say whether what he is displaying openly is a forbidden urge[2] or a conventionality; it seems that he would not have shied away from showing and permitting an artist to memorialize a desire that other sick people keep in the recesses of the mind or entertain in secrecy.

Smenkhkare was a handsome youth, and at an early age he was married to Meritaten, the eldest daughter of Nefretete. Having married the heiress, Smenkhkare was destined to inherit the throne. The second daughter, Meketaten, died young and was buried in the royal mausoleum in Akhet-Aton. The third daughter, Ankhesenpaaten, was married to her half brother Tutankhamen, but not before she was visited in her bridal chamber by her father, Akhnaton; the fruit of this union was a little girl who died soon after her birth.[3] The discovery of this fact concerning Akhnaton diminished the choir of acclaim that was heard in scientific, lay, and religious circles whenever the name of the great reformer and monotheist was pronounced.

Amenhotep III, one generation earlier, had also casually wed one of his daughters. Akhnaton followed his example. The influence of the Mitannian code of marital relations could have been responsible for these liberties unknown in the royal house of Egypt in earlier generations, prior to intermarriages with the royal house of Mitanni.

The union of Akhnaton with his daughter may be the basis

[2] In an ancient version of the Oedipus legend, Oedipus loved Chrysippus and killed his father Laius as a rival. Scholium to Euripides' *The Phoenissae*, 60.

[3] H. Brunner, *Zeitschrift für Aegyptische Sprache*, LXXIV (1938), 104–8. Ch. Desroches-Noblecourt in Claude F. A. Schaeffer, *Ugaritica III* (1956), pp. 204–5, 220.

of the ancient Greek tradition that, besides his mother-wife Jocasta, and the younger wife Euryganeia, who bore him several children and whom he sent away in disgrace, Oedipus wedded also a "virgin Astymedusa."[4] Students of ancient lore wondered at this complicated order of events[5]; the Greek tragedians, however, omitted these traditional elements to make the story great in its tragic simplicity: Oedipus lived with his mother as his spouse and queen. So did Akhnaton.

As the years went by the great empire—it never was greater or more luxuriantly abundant than in the days of Amenhotep III—started to crumble. Letters continued to arrive from Syria and Palestine with complaints and countercomplaints by princes and kings of the dependencies asking for military help against the bellicose king from the north, who was making deep incursions, against bands from the desert that crossed the Jordan and sacked the settlements there, and against one another. One of the vassal correspondents in Syria-Palestine wrote to the pharaoh:

"Listen to me. Why hast thou held back, so that thy land is taken? . . . Let not such things be said in future days, 'And thou wast not able to rescue it. . . .' "[6]

At another time he wrote: "If there is not a man to deliver me out of the hand of the enemy, and we—the regents—are put out of the lands, then all the lands will unite with the pillagers. . . . And if the king should then march forth all lands would be hostile to him, and what could he do for us then?"[7]

The el-Amarna letters give a vivid picture of the disintegra-

[4] Bethe, *Thebanische Heldenlieder*, pp. 23, 26.

[5] C. Robert, *Oidipus* (1915), I, 109ff.

[6] Mercer, *The Tell el-Amarna Tablets*, Letter 83.

[7] Ibid., Letter 74.

tion of the state. Not even a few score archers could be dispatched from Egypt. The faithful vassal wrote to el-Amarna:

"I in my solitude protect my right. . . . What should I do? Hear! I beg: refuse not. There are people in the presence of the king, or there are not? Hear me! Behold, so have I written to the palace; but thou hast not hearkened."[8]

Besides this falling away of the Asian provinces won in the campaigns of Akhnaton's predecessors, other signs of disintegration of the state, or displeasure of the gods, probably showed themselves in Egypt proper: it could have been famine, as in Palestine, of the repeated occurrence of which many letters bitterly complained; or epidemics, as in Cyprus, that depopulated the country and terrified its king, who wrote pathetic letters.

The nobles and the priests and the army could not look complacently on this disintegration of the empire, which also meant that the sources of revenue that filled Egypt with gold and other treasures from the dependent states were drying up. The people of Egypt must have regarded the disaster as punishment for some iniquity, and certainly the dispossessed priests of Amon, once immensely rich and now almost destitute, must have strengthened the populace and the nobles in the belief that a sin had been committed and had to be atoned for. This interpretation of the causes of a natural disaster or of a state catastrophe is entirely within the spirit of the ancient world. When a plague occurred in the days of King David, it was because he had made the mistake of counting the people; Solomon's kingdom was rent in twain soon after he died because of his sin of worshiping foreign gods; Saul did not do as the prophet had told him to and the prophet declared that the crown would not remain in his house.

The legend of Oedipus tells of some plague, famine, or other

[8] Ibid., Letter 122.

unidentified disaster[9] that visited the kingdom, on account of which it was decided to ask the oracle for the cause of the heavenly wrath in order to remove it or propitiate it. Similarly, at the end of Akhnaton's reign the land was plagued by some distress and Tutenkhamen so described it on a stele: *The land was sick and the gods turned their backs upon this land.*

The distress in which Egypt found itself by the end of Akhnaton's reign, must have been attributed by the priests or oracle of Thebes to the iniquity of their king. Darkness came where there had been light, privation where there had been riches, frivolity where there had been chastity, a curse where there had been a blessing. The throne of the son of Ra, the usual title of the pharaohs, was occupied by a sinful king.

Without a strong leader in the capital and at court, the priests would have been rather powerless after almost two decades of persecution. This strong leader arose now in the person of Ay, the king's brother-in-law. The same pattern prevailed in Boeotian Thebes in the events leading to the dethronement of King Oedipus of the swollen feet. Creon, the queen's brother, was the leader in the movement against the king, a movement he initiated and brought to a conclusion successful for him, disastrous for the king. "Creon" in Greek means merely "ruler." Ay, strong-willed like his sister Tiy, and like her ambitious and covetous of power, allied himself with the discontented and unfrocked Theban priesthood and worked for the restoration of the old faith and cult of Amon. His own sepulchral chambers in Akhet-Aton remained unfinished; the great hymn to Aton adorns the wall of one of these chambers, now deserted, the owner of the tomb having reverted to Amon.

[9] Marie Delcourt (*Stérilités mystérieuses et naissances maléfiques dans l'antiquité classique* [1938]) points out that Sophocles did not specify the nature of the disaster that befell Thebes; she presents arguments to show that by the plague of the legend was meant sterility, or barrenness of women, accompanied by the barrenness of cattle and fields.

The Blind Seer

To DETHRONE a king in Egypt, where he was godlike in the eyes of the people, all the forces of heaven and earth had to be conjured. In Boeotian Thebes the blind and merciless seer Tiresias contributed heavily to the king's downfall.

This blind prophet played a conspicuous role in the entire Theban cycle; he was the wise man and the divine seer to whom the past and the future were revealed. Among the Greeks and their legendary heroes there was no one at any time who equaled Tiresias as a seer. He was an old man in the days of Oedipus and his sons, and he was dead in the days of the following generation, that of the Trojan War; Odysseus went to Hades to consult him.

When the plague fell on the city of Thebes, Oedipus called on the blind seer to find out from him the cause of the gods' displeasure. The seer knew the truth: the plague had been sent as a punishment on the city that had among her people a parricide who lived in sin. At first the seer refused to divulge what he knew, but when accused by the king of plotting against him in conspiracy with Creon, he revealed a part of the truth. In the days of the struggle between the heirs of Oedipus, too, Tiresias, a powerful speaker and a diviner with inner sight, a gift of the gods, browbeat Creon for refusing burial to a fallen prince.

Tiresias was a seer but not an oracle; the oracle of Delphi was also called on to reveal the truth, and through these two, the priestly Pythia of Delphi and the blind seer, the gods let the mortals know their fate—more properly, their doom.

In the days of Amenhotep III and Akhnaton there lived in Egypt a man who was regarded as holy and as the wisest Egyptian, Amenhotep, son of Hapu, a seer and not a priest. After his death he was deified. Only one other person, Imhotep, not of royal status, and in a much earlier age, that of the Old Kingdom, was ever deified in Egypt. The autobiography of Amenhotep, son of Hapu, is so full of enigmatic statements that no one has yet tried to translate it from the Egyptian, except for a few pages with an exposition of his accomplishments in the civil field in the earlier part of his life. "Because of his wisdom and his alleged ability to foresee coming events, he was held to be a divine nature."[1] So was Tiresias of the legend.

Tiresias was familiar with the circumstances of Oedipus' birth and exposure. Therefore it is interesting that a passage among esoteric sentences of the Egyptian seer's autobiography refers to his being "intimate with the secrets of the royal nursery."

A portrait of Amenhotep, son of Hapu, has come down to us as a young person with long hair arranged not unlike that of the womenfolk of the time. If the seer was the prototype of Tiresias, this remarkable portrait, which made archaeologists wonder, may explain a curious detail in the Greek legend of Tiresias. The legend says that Tiresias once killed a female snake and in punishment was turned for a time into a woman. When he again became a man Zeus and Hera, who disputed whether a man or a woman has more pleasure from love-making, turned to Tiresias to ask him, since he had experience of both sexes. For saying that a woman has more enjoyment in inter-

[1] George Steindorff and Keith C. Seele, *When Egypt Ruled the East* (1957), p. 77.

AMENHOTEP, SON OF HAPU. *(Cairo Museum)*

TUTANKHAMEN. *(Louvre)*

SMENKHKARE. *(Berlin Museum)*

SMENKHKARE AND MERITATEN. LIMESTONE. *(Berlin Museum)*

TUTANKHAMEN AND ANKHESENPAATEN. *(Cairo Museum)*

TUTANKHAMEN AND ANKHESENPAATEN. FROM TUTANKHAMEN'S TOMB.
(Cairo Museum)

MERITATEN'S HEAD. FROM TOMB OF QUEEN TIY. *(Metropolitan Museum of Art)*

PANEL FROM THE CANOPY SHOWING QUEEN TIY IN GOLD FOIL. FROM
TOMB OF QUEEN TIY

COFFIN IN THE SEPULCHRAL CHAMBER OF QUEEN TIY. *(Tomb of
Queen Tiy)*

course, ("If the parts of love-pleasure be counted as ten, thrice three go to women, one only to men"[2]), Hera blinded him, but Zeus, to reward him, gave him long life to see the seventh generation and the gift of divination.

For a reason that has escaped the understanding of students of Egyptology, the deified seer Amenhotep was regarded as the patron of the blind, and this was so for many centuries down to the time of the Ptolemies.[3] It is conjectured that when this Amenhotep was alive he treated blind persons for their affliction. It seems more probable that he was made the patron of the blind because he himself became blind.

If we were to look for the historical Tiresias, the blind seer, a very old wise man, in the days of our historical setting, we would select Amenhotep, son of Hapu. Actually there is no one else who fills the role of a venerated seer in the days of Amenhotep III and his son Akhnaton. We do not know how long he lived; the only clue we have is that he reached his eightieth year in the thirty-fourth year of Amenhotep III, one or two years before the latter's death.[4] In order to live to the end of Akhnaton's reign, the seer must have reached the venerable age of ninety-eight. This rarely attained age is also implied in the other gift to the blind seer—great longevity.

A mortuary temple was erected for Amenhotep the Seer among those of the great kings, and he himself composed the text to be carved on its walls. His mortuary temple being situated below the cliffs that hide the Valley of the Kings, his grave must have been in that valley too. His sarcophagus has been found. It was an unusual distinction to have a grave and a

[2] Robert Graves, *The Greek Myths* (1955), II, 11. Apollodorus III, 71–72.

[3] H. Wild, "Ex-voto d'une princesse saïte à l'adresse d'Amenhotep fils de Hapu," in *Mitteilungen des Deutschen Instituts für aegyptische Altertumskunde in Kairo*, XVI (1958), 406–13.

[4] W. C. Hayes, *Journal of Near Eastern Studies*, X (1951), 100.

mortuary temple among the kings. In el-Amarna no tomb was prepared for him; apparently he did not leave Thebes for el-Amarna; and it seems that he was pro-Theban and pro-Ay, or pro-Creon as Sophocles presented him in *Oedipus Rex*.

In the face of national disaster, under the conditions then prevailing in Egypt, one could not fail to seek the counsel of the wise Amenhotep, son of Hapu; and since he had remained in Thebes when the king and the court moved to el-Amarna, we may guess what his stand was. The pitiless seer Tiresias was actually instrumental in the king's downfall, acting in concert with Creon.

That the misfortune that befell the crumbling empire was interpreted as a punishment from heaven meted out to the nation for the iniquity of their king is not a surmise. "When Tutankhamen describes Egypt troubled by the religious revolution of Amenophis IV [Akhnaton], he remarks that the disapproval of the gods was manifested by the failure of the military enterprises. 'If people were sent to the coast of Phoenicia to enlarge the frontiers of Egypt, they could in no wise succeed in this.' The failure of these enterprises was a sign of the anger of the gods."[5]

From the el-Amarna letters we know that there was no question of enlarging the frontiers; the question was whether the last Asian dependencies could be held under the Egyptian scepter.

Tutankhamen also wrote: "The gods, they had turned their back on this land . . . if one besought a god with a request for any thing, he did not come at all."[6] And Tiresias spoke similarly of the gods' refusing, because of a crime committed, to accept sacrifice and give an oracular answer. "The gods no more accept prayer and sacrifice at our hands" (*Antigone*).

[5] Jean Capart, *Thebes* (1926), p. 111.

[6] Steindorff and Seele, *When Egypt Ruled the East*, p. 224.

The anger of the gods had to be appeased. Akhnaton was in disfavor with the gods and with the great seer. Smenkhkare was won over to Ay's side. He was made to understand that in siding with Akhnaton he was actually supporting any claims Beketaten might have as heiress to the throne, to the detriment of the already exercised rights of Meritaten, his spouse. Earlier, Smenkhkare had ordered the name of Nefretete erased and replaced on monuments with the name of Meritaten, her daughter; then he changed his policy and turned against Akhnaton. It is known that he visited Thebes to make peace with the priests there. Before long Smenkhkare was alone on the throne and Akhnaton was deposed.

It is generally accepted that Akhnaton was deposed, and the idea has been repeatedly expressed that he went into exile.[7] But it is also assumed that for a period of time he continued to live in one of the residences in Akhet-Aton, a virtual prisoner. At the same time it is noted that the change took place without a revolution or insurrection.

An identical situation is found in the Boeotian Thebes of the legend. For a time Oedipus continued to live in his capital, though no longer a free suzerain.[8]

The bedouins who live a semi-nomadic life in mud huts in el-Amarna, the site of the ancient Akhet-Aton, have for decades been hired for excavation work by successive expeditions. When the double wall with a room over the gate was excavated north of the city, in the rear of which the prison-residence was located, the bedouins told the excavators that a doomed prince had been secluded there because his father wished to save him from the fate foretold at his birth.

[7] *"Die äusseren Umstände legen die Vermutung nahe, dass Echnaton gewaltsam beseitigt worden ist."* K. Lange, *König Echnaton und die Amarna-Zeit* (1951), p. 108.

[8] "Oedipus . . . was compelled by his sons always to remain in retirement, and the young men took over the throne, agreed together that they should reign in alternative years." Diodoros, trans. Oldfather.

These bedouins are illiterate and certainly do not know how to read hieroglyphs. It is interesting that in ancient Egyptian literature there is preserved a tale of the "Foredoomed Prince."[9] The oracle revealed that he would die a predestined death. The prophecy was made to the king, his father, before the son was born, a beginning not unlike the setting of the oracular prophecy made to King Laius. "Local tradition has attributed to this wall a version of the story—nearly contemporary with the city—of the Doomed Prince. . . . This wall, says the modern story-teller, was built by the King, his father, to protect him and to keep out his fate. Since we excavated it, however, the names have been added. The prince has become Tutankhamen [the discovery of his tomb in Thebes made that name familiar to all] and his father King Till—presumably the eponymous hero of the modern village of Et-Till. So are folk-stories made."[10]

Pendlebury did not suspect that the word "made" is not the perfect one in this case: seemingly some other "foredoomed prince" lived in that prison-palace. Akhnaton was an inmate of that place, and a few years earlier it had been occupied by Nefretete.

[9] *Journal of Egyptian Archaeology*, XI (1925), 227–29.

[10] Pendlebury, *Tell el-Amarna*, p. 44–45. The name Tell el-Amarna is a composite invented by the early archaeologists of the site; it was derived from the names of two bedouin tribes whose settlements were on the soil covering the ruins of Akhet-Aton, Amarna and Till or Tel. The latter contributed to some confusion, since Tell el-Amarna sounds as though there is a tell, or mound, but there is none.

The Blind King

Accoording to Euripides' version of the legend, Oedipus, after his removal from the throne, lived a blind man in a secluded prison-palace in Thebes. But according to Sophocles, Oedipus, having blinded himself when he found out the cruel truth, lived for some time in his palace, a deposed king, and then, a blind and broken man, was expelled from Thebes by his sons, actually during the reign of the elder son. All versions agree that he was blind.

Is there any evidence that Akhnaton became blind? Let us first put the question thus: is there any tradition that one of the pharaohs was blind? And in order that the analogy with Oedipus should not be a matter of mere chance, is there any tradition that a blind pharaoh was driven into exile? This would be in harmony with Sophocles' version (confirmed by a multitude of other authors who tell of Oedipus' exile), which is closest to the original version of the tradition.

Herodotus, in his history of Egypt, a part of his general history, says that in the line of pharaohs there "reigned a blind man called Anysis of the town of that name." Of him Herodotus reports that he fled into the marshes and was superseded by invaders, the Ethiopians. After fifty years the blind king was recalled to the throne from his exile in the marshland.

Tutankhamen is shown on a painting in his tomb as fighting

the Ethiopians. Thus a war with the Ethiopians in the days of Akhnaton's heirs is a historical fact. Another important detail preserved in Herodotus is that the name of the blind pharaoh who went into exile and the name of his city were identical. King Akhnaton called his capital by a name so similar to his own that even a modern Assyriologist wrote: "A new city, bearing the king's name, was erected."[1] Akhet and Akhn are derivatives of the same root, and Aton (Aten) is the same in both the name of the king and that of his capital. Herodotus rendered the names Akhnaton and Akhet-Aton as Anysis, one of the better transliterations of Egyptian names by Greek authors. The exact reading of the name is still a matter of surmise and Maspero, for instance, read the name of the king as Khuniatonu.

In an ancient Greek version of the legend an island of dunes was the place of Oedipus' exile;[2] this is not too different from a marshland, place of exile of the blind pharaoh.

Herodotus visited Egypt between the years 450 and 440 before the present era. He collected his information from priests who combined their temple duties with those of scribes and tourist guides. Herodotus has often been accused of having written a most unreliable account, but voices have also been heard in his defense.[3] The effort made in *Ages in Chaos* to discover the correct order of centuries and dynasties in many instances rehabilitates the "father of history." Herodotus' King Anysis occupied the throne of Egypt toward the end of the dynasty which is known as the Eighteenth; he was blind, he went into exile, and these are also major circumstances in the life of Oedipus, king of Thebes.

[1] R. W. Rogers, *Cuneiform Parallels to the Old Testament*, p. 257.

[2] Bethe, *Thebanische Heldenlieder*, p. 157.

[3] W. Spiegelberg, *The Credibility of Herodotus' Account of Egypt in the Light of the Egyptian Monuments* (1927).

Is there any contemporary evidence that Akhnaton became blind?

"Although a man sees the facts, yet the two eyes of the king, my lord, do not see . . ."—words written to Akhnaton in a letter by a vassal king in Palestine[4]—may not have been intended to refer to a physical disability, but in this case they were prophetic.

In the hymn that Akhnaton composed in praise of Aton and the daily wonders of the daybreak and the metamorphosis of the world and all that fills it at nightfall, there was an exuberant joy in the ability to see and a deep thankfulness for the gift of eyesight: "Eyes see beauty until thou settest. . . ."

When Akhnaton was deposed and the kingdom soon thereafter reverted to the faith of Amon, the nation was called on to pray and to render praise to the god restored to his former dominance and to despise and deride Akhnaton, the beloved hero of yesterday, the hated apostate of today. A hymn was composed, which pupils copied on inexpensive clay sherds. This hymn was written when Tutankhamen and Ay reigned.

> The sun of him that knew thee not hath set, O Amun.
> But he that knoweth thee, he shineth.
> The forecourt of him that assailed thee is in darkness,
> while the whole earth is in sunlight.
> Whoso putteth thee in his heart, O Amun,
> lo, his sun hath risen.[5]

A. Erman, the German Egyptologist who translated the hymn, looked for a meaning for the word "*weba*" that is written in hieroglyphs with the sign of an eye, and, not being prepared to think that Akhnaton became blind, translated it

[4] El-Amarna Tablet 288.

[5] A. Erman, *The Literature of the Ancient Egyptians* (1927), pp. 309–10.

"forecourt," as is usually done, explaining: "The buildings of the heretic, in particular el-Amarna."

All the world is in sunlight, the world of one man is dark: this is the meaning of the sentence, and "sight" is here intended by the use of the hieroglyph with a human eye.

Dr. Walter Federn, the learned Egyptologist who gave me this answer to my question as to whether in the literature contemporaneous with Akhnaton there is an indication that he became blind, added: "Moreover, *weba maa,* which Grapow in his work on medicine in ancient Egypt[6] translates 'to open (*weba*) the sight faculty (*maa*)' is the specific term of the Egyptian physicians for the treatment of eye diseases. So also Lefébvre, in his *Essai sur la médicine égyptienne de l'époque pharaonique* (1956), p. 87: '*Toute une série de remèdes sont encore indiqués pour "ouvrir la vue"* [*weba maa*], *ou simplement "améliorer la vue."*' Ebbell, in his translation of the *Ebers Papyrus* (1939), says rather colorlessly: 'Improve the sight.'"

Akhnaton became blind. He was not blind when he was on the throne, because then he would not have composed his hymn about the beauty of creation and would not have had so many statues made of himself. But in his adversity and disrepute he was blind. When all creation was filled with joy the sinner of Akhet-Aton groped in darkness. The height from which he fell made his misery the more painful and tragic. The king who wrote of himself and of his god, "Since thou didst establish the earth, thou hast raised them [men live] for thy son who came forth from thy limbs, the king living in truth," now is described as immersed in darkness "while the whole earth is in sunlight."

"The double lash of thy mother's and thy father's curse shall one day drive thee from this land in dreadful haste, with darkness then on the eyes that now can see true," the blind seer

[6] Grapow, *Grundriss der Medizin der alten Aegypter,* III (1956), 23.

said to the king: like himself, the king will "feel the ground before him with his staff."[7]

Would it be a flight of poetic imagination to assume that Akhnaton blinded himself by his own hand? It is possible that blindness developed as part of the syndrome, or combination of symptoms, of his organic malformation, and it could be regarded as a punishment for iniquity, and even as a self-inflicted punishment. But, with his highly neurotic character, a deep grief could have driven him to self-mutilation.

When Akhnaton built Akhet-Aton he made a vow to remain there to the end of his days. He also put his will on a boundary stele and asked the people of the city to do him justice and to entomb his body, and those of Nefretete and his eldest daughter, Meritaten, after their deaths, in the royal sepulcher of his capital. It was cut out of the rock, away from the tombs prepared for the nobles, at a site four miles into the desert. Its clearance by European archaeologists in the service of the Egyptian government in the last century is not one of the illustrious chapters of archaeological work. Only a brief report was published, "a summary description of the equally summary clearance."[8]

In one of the chambers of the tomb are pictures of the royal family in mourning for Meketaten, the second daughter, who died young. Actually she is the only person who is known to have been entombed in Akhet-Aton; except for her, neither the royal tomb nor the tombs of the nobles contain any sign that mortuary remains were deposited in any of them.

"There were found parts of Akhnaton's magnificent alabaster canopic chest with protecting vultures at the corners, together with pieces of the lids capped with the king's head. The chest

[7] Sophocles, *Oedipus Rex*, trans. Jebb.

[8] Bouriant et al., *Monuments du culte d'Atonou*, I (1903). No further volumes were published.

gives evidence of never having been used, for it is quite un-
stained by the black resinous substance seen in those of Amenophis II and Tutankhamen."[9]

Akhnaton's great yearning to lie in the hallowed ground he
had chosen was never fulfilled. One morning when the solar
disk rose over the horizon it shone on a man, yesterday a king,
now a wanderer going into exile.

It is worth noting that the self-glorifying Akhnaton's hymn
was found engraved in the tomb prepared for Ay in Akhet-Aton,
and certain historians have credited Ay with its authorship, for
he was then a devoted follower of Akhnaton, whom he later
opposed. Creon also was at first instrumental in raising Oedipus
to the heights and then pulling him down, blind and crownless.

In the lists of pharaohs composed by their successors, later
pharaohs, Akhnaton and his heirs are omitted, as though his
reign, personality, and progeny had been so evil that mere mention of them in writing was to be avoided. Where it was necessary to refer to Akhnaton, the words "that criminal of Akhet-
Aton" were substituted for his name. The word in Egyptian
carries the connotation of moral depravity and sinfulness.[10]

Oedipus, too, was first adored and later branded a sinner by
his townspeople, though in the Greek version of the tragedy
the sin of the king was committed by him unknowingly.

The end of Akhet-Aton was sudden. Smenkhkare moved to
Thebes. The houses were abandoned, and their inhabitants de-
parted by river and by land for Thebes or wherever they chose.
Those buildings that were not yet finished were left as they were;

[9] J. D. S. Pendlebury, "Report on the Clearance of the Royal Tomb
at El-Amarna," *Annales du Service des Antiquités de l'Egypte*, XXXI
(1931), 124.

[10] "In the great royal lists recording on the monuments the names of all
the past kings of Egypt, the name of Ikhnaton [Akhnaton] never appears;
and when under later Pharaohs, it was necessary in a state document to
refer to him, he was called 'the criminal of Akhetaten.'" J. H. Breasted,
The Dawn of Conscience (1933), p. 307.

in one of the houses, so near completion that only a block of stone remained to be placed above the entrance, the block was abandoned nearby and the builders departed. It was a hurried exodus. The houses, bare of furnishings, were left to decay.

As we have said, in none of the tombs of the nobles has any sign of occupancy been found. If any of them was used for the purpose of burial, the dead were removed to other localities when the population fled. Not even a cemetery for the common people was found. "The greatest mystery: Where is the cemetery?"[11] The entire population of the cemeteries, sparse as it must have been since the city had so short a life span, was removed by the authorities from the unhallowed ground of Akhet-Aton.

After some time wreckers came and executed the order to demolish the temple Akhnaton had built; they broke it into the smallest fragments. Some of the other public buildings were demolished that way too. None of them, upon excavation, was found to have walls higher than two or three feet above the foundations.

After a short history of less than fifteen years the capital, built for eternity, to last as long as the sun above the earth, became a ghost city of ruins, deserted even by the dead. Then sand covered the debris.

[11] Pendlebury, *Tell el-Amarna*, p. 166.

PART II

"A Ghastly Sight of Shame"

In 1907, in the Valley of the Kings near Thebes on the Nile, Theodore M. Davis, "having exhausted the surrounding sites," faced a small area in which "there was no sign of the probability of a tomb." Davis was an American from Rhode Island, a businessman who, through a chance visit to Egypt, became enthusiastic over the search for undiscovered tombs in the valley and obtained the required concession from the government to excavate. By 1907 he had already cleared several royal tombs, which he usually found had been emptied by earlier unlicensed diggers and tomb robbers in ancient times. But it was he who had opened the tomb of Yuya and Tuya, Queen Tiy's parents, undisturbed and intact.

The area he faced now was covered with limestone chips, possibly the dumpings of the surrounding tombs of Seti and Ramses I, II, III, and IX. "It seemed to be a hopeless excavation, resulting in a waste of time and money. Nevertheless, it had to be cleared whatever the result." In the course of several days Davis and his co-workers found nothing but chipped stone. "But down we went some thirty feet, when we found stone steps evidently leading to a tomb." Clearing the steps as they descended, Davis discovered the lintel of a door. "It had been closed with large and small stones. . . . The clearing of the door, so that we could enter, was soon done, when we found that

129

within a few feet of the door the mouth of the tomb was filled with stones to within four feet of the roof." On this pile of stones were lying, where they had been thrown, two wooden doors with copper hinges. "The upper faces of the doors were covered with gold foil marked with the name and titles of Queen Tiyi [Tiy]: It is quite impossible to describe the surprise and joy of finding the tomb of the great queen and her household gods, which for 3,000 years had never been discovered."[1]

Davis crawled along on the heap of stones through the narrow space under the ceiling of the passage and seventy feet from the mouth of the tomb came to a chamber rudely hewn in the rock. The objects found in the cavern were strewn around in the greatest disorder. The first thing that attracted the attention of Davis, probably because the light that was brought in fell first on them, were canopic jars, four in number. Canopic jars were used in Egypt for preserving the intestines and other inner organs of the deceased whose body was mummified. The jars in this tomb were alabaster, of exquisite workmanship, and their lids carried identical carved likenesses: these were beautifully executed heads, with open eyes, the irises and pupils inlaid with dark stone. The jars had been engraved with the name of their owner; however, every inscription had been carefully chiseled away and the name could not be read. Inside the jars were fabrics that had once been soaked in bitumen, but no remains of any viscera, which had completely decayed.

On the floor lay more gold-covered "doors" inscribed with the name of Queen Tiy; it was realized, though not immediately, that these "doors" were but the sides of the catafalque in which the coffin had been enclosed. One of the panels on the floor, partly covered with rubbish, had engraved in its foil the figure of the queen: she was pictured in a thin, transparent tunic, showing all the contours of her body; in front of her and facing

[1] Davis, *The Tomb of Queen Tiyi.*

in the same direction was Akhnaton, but his figure had been rudely hacked out of the gold foil.

The coffin was also there. "On the floor near by lay the coffin made of wood, but entirely covered with gold foil and inlaid with semiprecious stones. . . . Evidently the coffin had either been dropped or had fallen from some height, for the side had burst, exposing the head and the neck of the mummy. On the head plainly appeared a gold crown encircling the head, as doubtless it was worn in life by a probable queen. Presently we cleared the mummy from the coffin and found that it was a smallish person, with delicate head and hands. The mouth was partly open, showing a perfect set of upper and lower teeth. The body was enclosed in mummy-cloth of fine texture, but all of the cloth covering the body was of a very dark color. Naturally it ought to be a much brighter color. Rather suspecting injury from the evident dampness I gently touched one of the front teeth, and alas! it fell into dust, thereby showing that the mummy could not be preserved. We then cleared the entire mummy, and found that from the clasped hands to the feet, the body was covered with pure gold sheets, called gold foil, but nearly all so thick that when taken in the hands, they would stand alone without bending. These sheets covered the body from side to side."

The presence of jewelry and gold foil on the catafalque, the coffin, and the mummy was a clear indication that tomb robbers had never visited the tomb. But the tomb was in extreme disorder, a condition in which the entombers could not have left it. There was also an enigma in the choice of a burial place for a great queen. Servants of Queen Tiy received as royal gifts sepulchers of incomparably better construction than that which was made for her. Their sepulchers were made according to an architectural plan; their walls were covered with beautiful bas-reliefs. Queen Tiy's was a rough cell in the rock, not adorned with pictures; it was a damp place, and desolation was its prevailing feature. The seeming haste with which the royal corpse had been entombed, the lack of precautions that resulted in the coffin's falling and breaking, if it was not thrown down purposely, the disorder in the tomb, all called for an explanation. No thief having ever entered the burial place, it must have been a clandestine burial performed by unskilled hands, but there still remained the question of why the catafalque had been broken and some parts of it placed upon the heaps of stones in the entrance corridor; and the erasures of the name of the deceased on the canopic vases did not make the problem easier to solve.

"We then took off the golden crown, and attempted to remove the mummy-cloth in which the body was wrapped, but the moment I attempted to lift a bit of the wrapping it came off in a black mass, exposing the ribs. We then found a beautiful necklace which is now in the Cairo Museum. It was around the neck and resting on the breast beneath the mummy-cloth."

The wrappings of the mummy were entirely removed, exposing the bones. "Thereupon, I concluded to have them examined and reported upon by two surgeons who happened to be in the Valley of the Kings. They kindly made the examination and reported that the pelvis was evidently that of a woman. Therefore, everyone interested in the question accepted the sex, and supposed that the body was doubtless that of Queen Tiyi."[2]

But soon thereafter the bones were sent to Dr. G. Elliot Smith, professor of anatomy, who had examined the mummies and their royal bones from most of the graves of the Valley of the Kings near Thebes. "Alas!" wrote Davis, "Dr. Smith declared the sex to be male. It is only fair to state that the surgeons were deceived by the abnormal pelvis and the conditions of the examination."

Professor Gaston Maspero, the noted Egyptologist who was

[2] Ibid., p. 3.

in charge of all Egyptian antiquities in his position as director
of antiquities of the government in Cairo, co-operated with
Davis in the investigation of the case. He studied the gold leaf
of the catafalque and the coffin and the inscriptions impressed
in gold. The catafalque was undoubtedly that of the queen.
Her name was engraved in the gold foil on the broken sides
and cover of the catafalque. There, too, as on the walls of Huya's
tomb in Akhet-Aton, she was called "King's Mother and Great
Wife of the King." But the coffin appeared to be Akhnaton's.
The gold foil covering the body carried hieroglyphs of poly-
chrome inlay. The name of the king was erased, but the royal
titles were intact, especially the words "living in truth" which
Akhnaton regularly placed before his cartouches. The interior
of the coffin was also covered with gold leaf. Down the middle
of the coffin and of the lid ran a single column of hieroglyphs
engraved in the wood; gold had been pressed over them to
receive the imprint. "The cartouches of the king have been
everywhere destroyed, but the epithet 'Living for the Truth' is
entirely peculiar to Khuniatonu [Akhnaton]," wrote Maspero.
Similarly, the column of hieroglyphs on the foil covering the
mummy carried the epithet adopted by Akhnaton.

The Egyptologist had before him the task of a detective with
a most confusing set of clues. Maspero put it this way:

"First of all it must be clearly understood that the vault
discovered by Davis is not a real tomb; it is a rough cell in a
rock which has been used as a secret burying-place for a mem-
ber of the family of the so-called Heretic Kings, when the re-
action in favor of Amon triumphed. The transfer of the mummy
from its original tomb at Thebes, or el-Amarna, was devised and
made in order to save it from the wrath of victorious sectarians."
Maspero thought that either Tutankhamen or Ay planned and
executed the secret burial—only these two pharaohs "are likely
to have been actuated by kind feelings for Akhnaton. . . ."
Whoever the person was who felt compassion for the deceased

and interred the mummy, "he succeeded in carrying it out secretly [as] is evident from the fact that, while the Tombs of the Kings were desecrated and plundered completely, this place, with its wealth of gold, remained concealed and untouched" until Davis opened it.[3]

With the air of a Scotland Yard officer, Maspero presented the case of a corpse in a tomb not its own.

"The whole furniture was still in [the tomb], ready to bear witness as to the name and rank of its owner. When subsequently tested, its evidence was both obscure and conflicting. Such of the small objects as were inscribed bore the name of Amenothes III [Amenhotep III] and of his wife Tiyi, proving that the set of tiny pots, boxes, tools, fictitious offerings in enamelled stone or glazed pottery were the property of the queen. The big catafalque, in which the body had been borne to its resting place on the day of the burial, belonged to the same lady, and its inscriptions state that King Khuniatonu [Akhnaton] 'had made it for the King's mother, great wife of the King, Tiyi.' So far, so good, and there seemed to be no possible ground for doubting that the tomb was Tiyi's; but when we came to examine the mosaic coffin and the sheets of gold in which the mummy was wrapped, we found that their legends asserted the mummy to be no other than Khuniatonu [Akhnaton] himself.

"Such being the facts," Maspero proceeded, "how are we to reconcile them and explain satisfactorily the presence of Akhnaton's body amidst Tiyi's furniture? This paradoxical combination may either have been made on purpose, or be the result of some mistake on the part of the persons who executed the transfer."

In the first case, the supposition would be that "the hiders wanted the people to believe that the body they were burying was Tiyi's in order to prevent any harm being done to the

[3] Ibid., p. xiii.

[body of the] king by some fanatical devotee of Amon." That is why Tiy's catafalque and her small furniture were used. "I must confess that I look on this explanation as being too far-fetched to hold good," admitted Maspero. "The second supposition seems to me to be nearer the truth: the mummies of the dead members of Khuniatonu's family must have been taken out of their tombs and brought over to Thebes all together . . . once there, they must have been kept quietly for a few days in some remote chapel of the Necropolis. . . . When the time came for each to be taken to the hiding place which had been prepared for them in the Biban el-Moluk [Valley of the Kings], the men who had charge of these secret funerals mixed the coffins, and put the son where the mother ought to have been." Thus Maspero concluded that Akhnaton's mummy was buried by mistake in the vault prepared for his mother Tiy.

In offering this solution, however, Maspero disregarded an important clue, one that was known to him, for he wrote: "Dr. Elliot Smith, who studied the skull minutely, pronounced it to be the skull of a man aged about 25 or 26 years. Whether or not he be right about the age is a matter for anatomists only to decide; there is evidence, however, that the body discovered in Davis' vault is that of a man, and that man was Khuniatonu, if we must accept the testimony of the inscriptions."[4]

Akhnaton at his death could not have been so young. He reigned for sixteen years, at least, and he was grown up when he entered upon his reign. "A note on the estimate of the age attained by the person whose skeleton was found in the tomb" by Professor Elliot Smith, Fellow of the Royal Society, was printed with Davis' report. Smith wrote:

"When these bones were sent to me for examination two years ago, I reported that they formed the greater part of the skeleton of a young man who, judged by the ordinary European stand-

[4] Ibid., p. xiv.

ards of ossification, must have attained an age of about 25 or 26 years at the time of his death." The archaeologists tried to find out whether the age of the deceased could have been higher. Could the dead have been thirty years old? "It is highly improbable that he could have attained thirty years if he had been normal."

Normal, however, the skeleton was not; the cranium exhibited "in an unmistakable manner the distortion characteristic of a condition of hydrocephalus." The numerous pictures and sculptures of Akhnaton and the members of his family with overly long heads apparently were based on a real deformity characteristic of him and his family, as is evident from the cranium of the mummy found by Davis. Later other anatomists stressed the fact that in hydrocephalus the frontal part of the cranium is extended but never the occipital part, as is the case with the cranium ascribed to Akhnaton, and an extension of this kind is not associated with retardation in the development of the bones.

Davis and Maspero published the account of the find—the tomb and its contents—as *The Tomb of Queen Tiyi*, and ascribed the body in the coffin to Akhnaton. But there was no answer to the question of why Tiy received such a humble sepulcher when her own parents, of common stock, were entombed in the same Theban necropolis in a richly furnished sepulcher; nor to the question of why Akhnaton was in the coffin and Tiy's body had disappeared; nor to the question of how it was that Akhnaton died so young.

Arthur Weigall, who after a while took Maspero's place as director of antiquities, joined Maspero in the belief that the body was that of Akhnaton. Mention has not been made here of the fact that in the rubbish of the tomb were found "foundation" bricks bearing the name of Akhnaton, and also royal seal impressions of Tutankhamen. A few bricks with the signet impression of Tutankhamen were found strewn on the floor among objects pertaining to Tiy. If Akhnaton reigned for sixteen or seventeen years, and was twenty-six years old at his death, he must have started his reign at the tender age of ten and introduced his religious reform and written his hymn to Aton, for which he is known as "the first monotheist," in his early teens. Some scholars accepted this scheme but ascribed to Tiy the initiative and the active part in the religious reform, and attributed the authorship of the hymn to Ay. But obviously such conjectures are very strained.

Before we leave the desolate burial cavern made for Queen Tiy and occupied by the corpse of an unknown young man, one more clue must be described. It is a prayer or a love song cut with a stylus in the gold foil under the feet of the mummy. It was not included in the Davis-Maspero report but was published and translated later. This song, or prayer, or word of parting, incised in the foil, reads:

> I inhale the sweet breeze that comes from thy mouth,
> I contemplate thy beauty every day.
> It's my desire to hear thy lovely voice
>   like the north wind's whiff.
> Love will rejuvenate my limbs.
> Give me thy hands that hold thy soul,
> I shall embrace and live by it.
> Call me by name again, again, forever,
>   and never will it sound without response.

In these beautiful words someone expressed a longing unconquered by death. It was a parting song of love to the deceased by a survivor. It was not written on the coffin, or on the golden sheet that covered the body, or on the pectoral; it was secreted under the feet of the dead. The name of the writer was erased.

These lines, when read, only intensified the mystery of the

tomb and the desire to know who the dead person in the royal coffin was and why he was there.

A ray of light came out of another grave, which held more than one mystery of its own.

TOMB OF TUTANKHAMEN. SHRINE I. *(Cairo Museum)*

TOMB OF TUTANKHAMEN. SHRINE III

A DETAIL OF SHRINE III

TUTANKHAMEN FIGHTING ENEMIES. PAINTING ON A CHEST, TUTAN-
KHAMEN'S TOMB. (*Cairo Museum*)

SECOND GOLD COFFIN OF TUTANKHAMEN. LID. *(Cairo Museum)*

THE INNERMOST GOLD COFFIN OF TUTANKHAMEN. *(Cairo Museum)*

GOLD MASK OF TUTANKHAMEN. *(Cairo Museum)*

VALLEY OF THE KINGS NEAR THEBES

PIT TOMB IN THE VALLEY OF THE KINGS

A KERCHIEF OF LINEN FOUND IN THE PIT TOMB. DRAPED ON A CAST OF THE HEAD OF A PRINCESS, DAUGHTER OF AKHNATON. *(Metropolitan Museum of Art)*

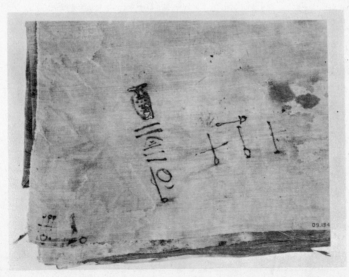

FINE LINEN FOUND IN THE PIT TOMB. INSCRIBED AND ORNAMENTED WITH HIEROGLYPHS WOVEN INTO CLOTH. *(Metropolitan Museum of Art)*

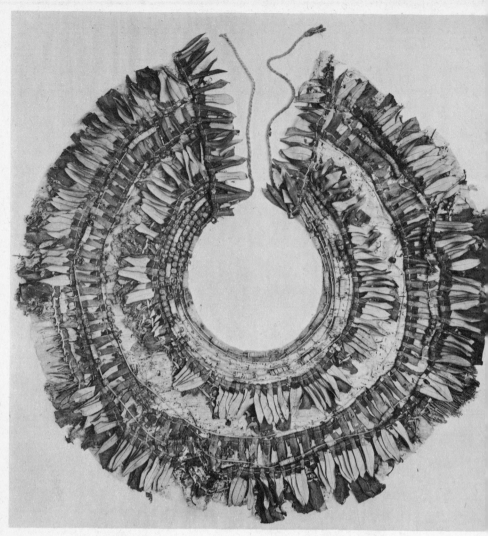

FLORAL COLLAR FROM THE PIT TOMB. *(Metropolitan Museum of Art)*

"Crowned with Every Rite"

No ARCHAEOLOGICAL find ever made has produced such widespread interest as the tomb of Tutankhamen. Neither the discovery of Nineveh and the library of Assurbanipal, nor those of Troy, the tombs of Mycenae, or the el-Amarna state archive of letters, to mention but a few highlights in the story of archaeology, made a comparable impression on the public of the world. No grave ever opened in Egypt contained even a semblance of the riches that Tutankhamen's grave held. Front-page reports in newspapers all over the world stirred up public interest and put all other news in the shade. The beer-hall putsch in Munich, even the earthquake and tidal wave that devastated Tokyo and other cities in Japan and took hundreds of thousands of lives, detracted for only a comparatively short period from the sustained interest in the discovery of Howard Carter in the Valley of the Kings near Thebes.

For several seasons Carter and his workers dug in the valley without any appreciable success. The digging was financed by Lord Carnarvon, a wealthy man, in whom interest in antiquities and the adventurous spirit of the traveler and sportsman united to make archaeology his main hobby when his health required that he stay away from the mists of his native England. Since the discovery of Theodore Davis in 1907, almost no important find had been made in the valley, and the concession to excavate was transferred to Carnarvon in 1914. A son of the fourth Earl of Carnarvon, who translated the *Agamemnon* and the Odyssey into English verse, George was impatient to earn the laurels of Schliemann, of whose discovery of Troy and the tomb of Agamemnon he must have heard a great deal in his childhood from his father. Several seasons of work brought nothing to Carter and Carnarvon except heaps of overturned stones, said to amount to two hundred thousand tons, and they decided to spend just one last season on the triangular lot on which they had done all their work before departing to another area, possibly outside the valley.

In November 1922, Carter discovered, underneath some laborers' huts dating from the Twentieth Dynasty, steps leading down and then a sealed door; one seal was that of Tutankhamen; the other was of the priests of the necropolis. Carter assumed that tomb robbers had entered the grave sometime before the Twentieth Dynasty and that the door had been resealed by the authorities in charge of the necropolis. A corridor was freed of the stones with which it had been filled to protect the tomb from violators; a layer of stones of a different color showed where the visitors had made their way inside. A sealed door, again with the original seal of Tutankhamen and with that of the priests, was encountered. What the eyes saw by the light of a torch through a hole which Carter made in the door was more than the poet of the Arabian Nights had invented for his treasure cave and more by far than any hoard of riches ever discovered by archaeologists. "Surely never before in the whole history of excavation had such an amazing sight been seen as the light of our torch revealed to us."[1] A golden throne, golden couches, a golden chariot, shrines, vases, statues—an unimaginable collection of treasures filled the place. "The furniture, which has never been surpassed in the perfection of its workmanship and ex-

[1] Carter and Mace, *The Tomb of Tut-ankh-Amen*, I (1923), 98.

quisite decoration; linen of a fineness and a beauty of texture
that have never been excelled; carved alabaster vases such as
the world has never seen before. . . . What is the meaning of
all this lavish display of skill and beauty? Why was so much
wealth poured into the hidden recess of this desolate ravine,
and the most exquisite products of the world's achievement in
the arts and crafts buried out of sight in this strange necropolis?"[2]

From this treasure room a sealed door led Carter and
Carnarvon to another room also filled with treasures; a concealed
second door opened into the shrine chamber. In it was a shrine
16 feet 6 inches long, 10 feet 9 inches wide, and 9 feet high,
which filled the chamber so that there was just room enough
for a man to squeeze his body through as he walked around
it. It was inlaid with costly designs of sparkling blue faience
with magic formulas for the protection of the dead king. When
the doors of the shrine were opened, there was a gold shrine inside the first, also of magnificent workmanship; and inside the
second shrine there was a third, likewise of gold and engraved all
around with hieroglyphs and designs and exquisitely made.[3]

The work of clearing the antechamber and the treasure room
of the riches in gold, jewels, precious stones, couches, thrones,
golden carriages, golden chests, and rich fabrics took weeks and
months. In the meantime Lord Carnarvon died of blood poison-
ing following a mosquito bite. He did not live to see the opening
of the third shrine. Inside this shrine, Carter expected, would
finally be the coffin, but instead he found there a fourth shrine
"even more brilliant in workmanship than the last." "With in-

[2] G. Elliot Smith, *Tutankhamen and the Discovery of His Tomb* (1923),
p. 45.

[3] Photographs of the various shrines, taken from all four sides, as
well as their description, are found in *The Shrines of Tut-Ankh-Amon*,
by A. Piankoff, ed. N. Rambova, Bollingen Series, XL, No. 2 (Pantheon
Books, 1955).

tense excitement I drew back the bolts of the last and unsealed doors and there, filling the entire area within . . . stood an immense yellow quartzite sarcophagus, intact, just as the pious hands had left it." Figures of goddesses protected the sarcophagus with wings and outspread arms. A lid of rose granite, weighing more than twelve hundred pounds, covered the sarcophagus, which had been cut from a single great block of yellow quartzite 8.8 feet long, 4.8 feet wide, and 4.8 feet high. When the lid was raised, there was a golden effigy of the king, and it shone as though it had been made the day before. Royal emblems of power were held in crossed arms. A tiny wreath of flowers, still with a little color in them, lay on the golden forehead. Beneath this golden "anthropoid" coffin was another golden coffin; on its lid the dead pharaoh was modeled in the figure of Osiris. Inside was a third coffin, 6 feet long, made of solid gold and very heavy. When it was opened, there finally was the mummy. Its head was covered with a "gold portrait mask of Tutankhamun. The mummy was richly decked with jewels, and every sort of trinket which had delighted the boy king in life was permitted to accompany him in the tomb at death." Gold sandals were on his feet, and each finger and toe had "its individual stall of gold. His fingers were resplendent with gold rings, many of which were adorned with scarabs engraved with the name of the king. Broad armlets graced his arms, while his neck and breast were heavy with tastefully fashioned and arranged chains, collars, pectorals, amulets, and beads of gold, semiprecious stones, and fayence." Every one of these articles was "an outstanding masterpiece of artistic workmanship and a magnificent credit to its creator."[4]

"The face was refined and cultured, the features well-formed, especially the clearly marked lips."[5] But the rest of the body,

[4] Steindorff and Seele, *When Egypt Ruled the East*, pp. 228–32.

[5] Carter, *The Tomb of Tut-ankh-Amen*, II, 113.

with the exception of the feet, was damaged, almost burned, through an excessive use of unguents by the embalmers. More than one hundred and forty pieces of jewelry were found between the wrappings of the mummy.

It was years before Carter, after carefully removing all the treasures (in the meantime he had found that there was also a fourth chamber, reached from the sepulchral hall, filled with chests and effigies and other splendors), and after dismantling the four shrines, opened the sarcophagus and the three golden coffins, in the last of which he found the mummy. After the swathes were cut through, the mummy was examined by Dr. D. E. Derry. The anatomist established the age of Tutankhamen at his death as between seventeen and eighteen years, closer to the second figure. He was struck by the similarity between the crania of Tutankhamen and the royal dead in the tomb found by Davis. Tutankhamen had the very same unusual thickening of the occipital bones, a characteristic clearly expressed on the numerous portraits of Akhnaton. Professor Derry arrived at the startling conclusion that Tutankhamen was a son of Akhnaton; until then he had been known to be a son-in-law of Akhnaton and husband of Akhnaton's third daughter by Nefretete, Ankhesenpaaten. If he was a son of Akhnaton, then, he was married to his sister or half sister.

The cranium and the bones of the man in Queen Tiy's grave were re-examined by Dr. Derry, who took over the chair of anatomy at Cairo University previously occupied by Elliot Smith. He concluded that the man in Akhnaton's coffin in Tiy's grave was no more than twenty-four years old, at the most, at his death, and more probably twenty-three. Professor Smith likewise reduced his estimate, writing in 1930: "The archaeological evidence seemed to leave no doubt that the bones were actually those of the heretic king, but a difficulty now arose from the consideration that the anatomical evidence seemed to point to an age of about 23. . . ."[6] His reservation, that in the event of hydrocephalus retardation in the growth of the epiphyses in the bones could occur and in that case the dead could have been a little older, was dismissed by Dr. Derry, who made it absolutely clear that the change in the cranial bones of the mummy was not caused by hydrocephalus. Dr. Derry posed the problem to an Egyptologist, Dr. Engelbach, for the purpose of having him re-examine all the evidence and find out whose body had been in the royal coffin in the secret cavern. Dr. Engelbach carried out the assignment successfully. He proved that the mysterious mummy was Smenkhkare. Tiy and Akhnaton and Tutankhamen were ruled out. The appellation "Who lives in truth," which remained intact before the erased cartouches on the coffin in which the body was found, was peculiar to Akhnaton; the expression repeatedly found on the gold foil covering the mummy, "Beloved of Akhnaton," would not identify the body as that of the heretic king but as that of one of whom Akhnaton was fond; and this expression is also found in other instances, always referring to Smenkhkare.[7] This solution was generally accepted by the authorities. The alabaster jar with a lid bearing a carved head, one of the precious possessions of the Metropolitan Museum of Art in New York, obtained as a gift from Davis, who found four such jars in the tomb of Tiy—the three others are in Cairo—was consequently also identified as that of Smenkhkare, and the likeness that had previously been identified by a sign reading first "Queen Tiy" and then "King Akhnaton" received a new sign: "Smenkhkare of the Eighteenth Dynasty."

By comparing the two skeletons of Tutankhamen and Smenkhkare Professor Derry established that they were broth-

[6] G. Elliot Smith, Introduction to *The Papyrus Ebers*, trans. from German version by C. P. Bryan, (1930), p. xxx.

[7] Actually, "Beloved of Neferkheperura Uaenra," which was the throne name of Akhnaton. *Annales du Service*, XXXI (1931), 105.

ers, both sons of Akhnaton. Carter, in his report on the tomb of Tutankhamen, told of Derry's establishment of the father-son relation between Akhnaton and Smenkhkare;[8] now the determination that Smenkhkare and Tutankhamen were brothers threw new light on the problem of the succession to Akhnaton's throne.

After Akhnaton ceased to reign, Smenkhkare occupied the throne for a short while. The latest date mentioned for him is the "third year," but it is assumed that the period of co-regency with his father is included, so that his reign alone may have been as much as a year but hardly more.[9] After a short reign he lost the throne to his brother under conditions that suggest a rivalry. Carter wrote in his report: "It is quite possible that he [Smenkhkare] met his death at the hands of a rival faction."[10] He proceeded: "Tut-ankh-Amen himself was little more than a boy. Clearly in the first years of this reign of children [he and his wife Ankhesenpaaten] there must have been a power behind the throne, and we can be tolerably certain who this power was . . . this was Ay, Chief Priest, Court Chamberlain . . . the most powerful court official. Now, looking ahead a little, we find it was this same Ay who secured the throne for himself after Tut-ankh-Amen's death. We also know, from the occurrence of his cartouche in the sepulchral chamber of the newly found tomb, that he made himself responsible for the burial ceremony of Tut-ankh-Amen. . . . It is quite unprecedented in the valley to find the name of a succeeding king upon the walls of his predecessor's sepulchral monument. The fact that it was so in this case seems to imply a special relationship between the two, and we shall probably be safe in assuming

[8] Carter, *The Tomb of Tut-ankh-Amen*, III, 18.

[9] G. Roeder, "Thronfolger und König Smench-ka-re," *Zeitschrift für Aegyptische Sprache*, LXXXIII (1958), Heft I, 45.

[10] Carter and Mace, *The Tomb of Tut-ankh-Amen*, I, 43.

that it was Ay who was largely responsible for establishing the boy king upon the throne. Quite possibly he had designs upon it himself already, but, not feeling secure enough for the moment, preferred to bide his time and utilize the opportunities he would undoubtedly have as minister to a young and inexperienced sovereign, to consolidate his position."[11]

But how could he have had designs on the throne occupied by one who was his junior by two generations unless he planned his charge's injury and death?

On the walls of the sepulcher of Tutankhamen, Ay had himself pictured as administering the mortuary rites to the young king. He thus stressed that he was the author of the funeral arrangements for the dead monarch; no other instance is known of a king who had himself portrayed as officiating at the funeral of his predecessor.[12]

The question as to why this monarch, who ruled only a very short time and died young, was honored to such an extent after his death was raised but could not be answered. One author wrote: ". . . curiously enough, for all the splendor of his burial,[13] Tutankhamen was a ruler of little importance." Carter, the discoverer of his tomb, wrote of him: "In the present state of our knowledge we might say with truth that the one outstanding feature of his life was the fact that he died and was buried. Of the man himself—if indeed he ever arrived at the dignity of manhood—and of his personal character we know nothing."[14] This quotation is from the first volume of the report, written before the shrines and the coffins had been opened and Dr.

[11] Ibid., pp. 43-44.

[12] "This scene is without precedent, a succeeding pharaoh never before or after being depicted in a former ruler's tomb." Penelope Fox, *Tutankhamun's Treasure* (Oxford University Press, 1951) p. 20.

[13] "The burial which is a pageant" (Ibid., p. 37).

[14] Carter and Mace, *The Tomb of Tut-ankh-Amen*, I, 45.

Derry had made the anatomical study on the mummy. Pictures in the tomb showed Tutankhamen shooting down rows of enemies and strafing prisoners of war. This detail, if not a piece of invention, which it probably is not, points to military action in Tutankhamen's reign. It is not inconceivable that he died young in war and that for this act of patriotism he received the honors of an exceedingly rich sepulcher and the privilege of having the next king pay him tribute on his death.

One cannot close one's eyes to the great difference in the appearance, arrangements, riches, and order—and disorder—in the tombs of the two brothers who ruled one after the other. For the younger brother, a gilded shrine covered with jewels containing within it three more shrines covered with gold, one inside another, a beautiful sarcophagus, and three coffins, the innermost one of solid gold; for the elder, a shattered shrine—called by Davis a catafalque—which had not been made for the deceased, and a coffin covered with gold foil that had fallen down and cracked, exposing a crumbling mummy, poorly swathed, whose head stuck out of the crack. But this miserable place, a hide-out and not a sepulcher, showed too that somebody had administered rites, albeit poorly: near Smenkhkare's body were found burnt herbs and incense. Somebody, too, had left a few flowers, turned to dust, and had written a song of love rarely excelled for beauty, and had hidden it at the feet of the dead. The disorder in the chamber must have been created by people who had come to violate the tomb and desecrate it, and who probably also erased names on the coffin and the broken shrine, and overturned the coffin but did not carry away the small amount of gold that was there.

When Oedipus abandoned the throne, compelled to do so by the crafty Creon, his uncle and also brother-in-law, who acted in reliance on the will of gods inimical to the king, two sons of Oedipus, Polynices and Eteocles, agreed to rule in turns.

They were both very young. Polynices, the elder of the two, reigned first; after a year he handed over the throne to Eteocles and left the kingdom, returning to claim the crown when it was his turn to reign again. However, Creon, the regent, encouraged the boy king to reject his brother's rightful claim and to keep the throne for himself. *The Seven against Thebes* is laid in the time when Eteocles was king of Thebes and his brother Polynices had come with an allied foreign host and was attacking the city.

> And strange is the Lord of Division, who cleaveth
> the birthright in twain . . . ,
> Dividing in bitter division the lot of the children
> of teen!
> Not the wide lowland around, the realm of their
> sire, shall they have,
> Yet enough for the dead to inherit, the pitiful
> space of a grave![15]

The Egyptian prototypes of the drama were Smenkhkare and Tutankhamen. They were brothers and Smenkhkare ruled first; he was presented in royal regalia when Akhnaton was still alive and on the throne, since they are shown on the same bas-relief. Akhnaton gave away his royal power in his lifetime, but Smenkhkare, who returned from Akhet-Aton to Thebes, ruled for only a short time, about a year, and at that time he was still in his teens.

Soon the throne of Thebes was occupied by Tutankhamen. Ay, Tiy's brother, acted as regent. It is understood that Smenkhkare lost his throne to his rival, his younger brother, who could not have acted as he did on his own but was supported and directed by the regent.

Thus we find again a very similar situation in Thebes in

[15] Aeschylus, *The Seven against Thebes*, trans. E. D. A. Morshead, in *The Complete Greek Drama*, ed. Oates and O'Neill, Jr.

Greece and in Thebes in Egypt. The king who lived in incest with his mother surrendered his power and after a while was sent away into exile. The young prince in whose reign he was exiled ruled only a short time and was replaced by his rival, a brother, also a youth in his teens. In both cases—in the legend and in history—the real power was concentrated in the hands of a royal relative, a maternal uncle, who preferred the younger prince—Eteocles in the legend, Tutankhamen in history.

The unknown war in which, according to the paintings in his tomb, Tutankhamen took part was apparently the war against his brother and the allied host he brought against Thebes.[16] Both died young, killed in that war.

[16] In these panels Tutankhamen wages war against Syrians and Ethiopians.

"A Tomb-Pit in the Rock"

CREON, the ruler of Thebes, decreed that one fallen prince should be buried with all honors and riches, the other left unburied; and it was announced to the people of Thebes:

"Eteocles, who hath fallen fighting for our city, in all renown of arms, shall be entombed, and crowned with every rite that follows the noblest dead to their rest. But for his brother, Polyneices, who came back from exile, and sought to consume utterly with fire the city of his fathers . . . none shall grace him with sepulture or lament, but leave him unburied, a corpse for birds and dogs to eat, a ghastly sight of shame."[1]

Royal rites were performed over the body of the young prince, the favorite of the all-powerful Creon, and he was borne to his grave in splendid armor and with all riches. To stress the disparity, the funeral rituals were carried out sumptuously, and the sepulcher was endowed munificently. The death penalty was decreed for whoever buried the other prince, Polynices. "The hapless corpse of Polyneices . . . none shall entomb him or mourn, but leave unwept, unsepulchred. . . ."[2]

The rich burial chamber for Tutankhamen and the poor hiding place for Smenkhkare, both of whom wore the crown of Egypt, are once more, in history and in legend, the lot of

[1] Sophocles, *Antigone,* trans. R. C. Jebb.

[2] Ibid.

the younger and the elder brothers. It was the regent, now himself king, who performed the rites for the deceased boy king; and as in the legend, so in history—documented by the paintings and inscriptions on the walls of Tutankhamen's tomb —the regent, the next king, Ay, "with no precedent known in the history of Egypt," had himself pictured in this role, displaying his great concern that a worthy tribute be rendered to the dead monarch.

Ay was anxious, too, that Smenkhkare should not have the mortuary honors due a king. Even if he was deposed, he was a prince of royal blood, and he had once worn the crown of Egypt. It appears that somebody hid him in the roughly hewn cell, burned a few boughs at the bier of the dead, made a hurried attempt to embalm the body, and showed great devotion to the dead prince.

Someone disobeyed the decree of the old regent-king, Creon, and "sought to hide the nakedness." It was Antigone, a sister of the fallen princes, who disregarded the regent's decree which, in her mind, conflicted with "unwritten and unfailing statutes of heaven." Secretly she covered the body of her apostate brother with dust, knowing that for this act of love and devotion she would forfeit her own life.

"I breathe thy sweet breath which comes forth from thy mouth. . . . It is my desire that I may hear thy sweet voice, even the north wind. . . . Give me thy hands. . . . Call thou upon my name even unto eternity and I shall never fail. . . ."

These words, as we know, are not from the sad dirges of Sophocles' *Antigone;* they are from the last love message left by the historical Antigone at the feet of her dead brother.

Antigone was apprehended and brought before the regent. She admitted that she could not bear to have her brother "lie in death an unburied corpse." Creon was merciless toward the princess who had defied his first decree as king.

"But verily, this too is hateful—when one who hath been

caught in wickedness then seeks to make the crime a glory," and he resolved that she "shall not avoid a doom most dire." He would not kill her nor would he let her live. She would be immured alive in a tomb-pit in the rock, with food placed there to sustain her life in agony, "no home with the living or with the dead. . . . I will take her where the path is loneliest, and hide her, living, in a rocky vault, with so much food set forth as piety prescribes, that the city may avoid a public stain."[3]

Euripides indicated that Antigone's pit-tomb was near the grave of her brother.

Antigone: "I will bury him although the state forbids."

Creon: "Do so, and thou wilt be making thine own grave near his."

The "tomb, bridal-chamber, eternal prison in the caverned rock," was near the place of her crime.

At the end of the report on *The Tomb of Queen Tiyi*, a tomb that we now know contained the body of Smenkhkare, Davis mentioned the following find, which did not merit a separate publication nor yet deserved to remain unrecorded:

"A short time ago, I found a small pit tomb three hundred feet from Tiyi's tomb. It was covered with rock and sand about three feet deep. It proved to be about seven feet square and six feet deep. It was filled with white jars sealed with covers." These jars "contained small red cups" and other objects "of little value." Davis conjectured that these objects had been removed from the tomb of some poor man "for the purpose of finding a tomb for Queen Tiyi" and that "it was the only one that could be found in the vicinity" for the storage of the removed containers. But to store the poor man's funeral vessels there was no need for a chamber seven feet square and six feet deep. And why should a poor man's tomb contain a multitude of white jars sealed with covers and many small red cups?

[3] Ibid.

As the find did not warrant a separate publication, Davis omitted to say whether bones of a skeleton were found in this grave; probably there were bones, otherwise Davis would have called the cell not a tomb but a cache. And if it was not a tomb, why were the jars of a poor man kept in the Valley of the Kings? Each of the cups could have originally contained some food.

That this place may have been the death chamber of the historical Antigone is no more than sheer surmise. We are moved to this conjecture by two or three considerations: the proximity of the place to the hidden tomb of the fallen king-pretender; the form of the rock cell, unusual in the Valley of the Kings; and the presence of jars and cups, apparently with food for many days or even months.

As her life was forfeit and she was expected to die it was proper, she having been born a princess, to prepare her death chamber in the Valley of the Kings, and since she had committed the crime of entombing her brother it was proper that she should die close by. Again, nothing but the many white jars and red cups permit even for a moment this surmise. And only as such does this idea find a place here. Having dealt with so many fantasies of the tragedians, may not we, too, play with this one of our own, and let it be discarded if the discriminating reader is unable to accept it?

This conjecture I leave here in its original form, though additional published material lends it an aspect of more than mere fantasy. Theodore Davis laconically described his find on less than a page added to the text of *The Tomb of Queen Tiyi*, and it was of that publication in general that Alan H. Gardiner almost half a century later complained:

"The history of excavation in Egypt presents, side by side with much splendid work, an almost continuous series of disasters. The greatest disaster of all is when the results have remained completely unpublished. But it is also a disaster when the publication is incomplete or inaccurate. This is unfortunately what has happened with Theodore M. Davis' volume. . . ."[4]

But Theodore M. Davis (not to be confused with Norman de Garis Davies, who described the tombs of el-Amarna) was not a learned archaeologist, if he was a learned man at all. He employed archaeologists to dig for him, paying for this from the proceeds of the Newport, Rhode Island, Casino, of which he was the controlling stockholder. He made a name as a patron of Egyptology; he died in 1915 on the estate of William Jennings Bryan in Florida.

In 1941 H. E. Winlock published a memoir[5] in the series of "Papers" of the Metropolitan Museum of Art in New York, to which Dr. Walter Federn, my erudite friend and a bibliographer in Egyptology, only recently drew my attention, saying that there I would find something more about the cache of pots and vessels in the pit in the Valley of the Kings. That January of 1908, when the cache was found, Winlock was in Thebes. When he published his memoir on the find, he was the lone survivor of those who had been present at the discovery; all the others had died in the following nine years. He recounted sarcastically that a British diplomat named in his paper wrote Mr. Davis a curious note "saying to Mr. Davis that he had heard that the latter's men found a royal tomb every winter and requested as he intended to be in the Valley of the Kings in a few days, that all discoveries be postponed until his arrival." Mr. Davis obliged as much as he could.

The pit cut in the rock was only one hundred and twenty yards from the place where later the tomb of Tutankhamen was found, on the south side of the eastern branch of the Valley of the Kings, and almost an equal distance—one hundred yards —from the place where Smenkhkare was abandoned in a dis-

---

[4] Gardiner, *Journal of Egyptian Archaeology*, XLIII (1957), 10.

[5] *Materials Used at the Embalming of King Tut-ankh-Amun*, Metropolitan Museum of Art Papers, No. 10 (1941).

ordered tomb. Winlock's description reveals that the pit with the pots and small vessels also contained remains of food and some cloth. Rejecting Davis' explanation ("No one in the Theodore Davis camp knew exactly what this mass of material was"), Winlock offered his own: the food was the remainder of a meal of which a group of people partook; the linen was the material used for embalming; certain finds in this pit testified that its contents had been placed there about the time when Tutankhamen was entombed or shortly thereafter, and Winlock concluded that those who partook of the meal were mourners for the king.

"The evidence of the date is clear." In the tomb were found six clay impressions of seals. Three of these impressions bear distinctly the cartouches of Tutankhamen. The fourth seal is that of the priests of the necropolis of the Valley of the Kings— a jackal above nine bound captives. It is the same seal that sealed the doors to the graves of Tutankhamen and Smenkhkare ("Tiy's tomb"). The linen cloths in the pit had marks painted on them in blue-black, and two of them gave a date, that of the last year of Tutankhamen. One sheet especially attracted the attention of Winlock. It is a large piece 2.44 meters (over 8 feet) long and 61 centimeters (over 2 feet) wide, from whose width a piece had been ripped off on each side. "The sheet is of very fine, tightly woven but not heavy linen, with 36 warp threads and 28 woof threads to the centimeter." It was "badly worn and stained in antiquity."

"The marks are among the most curious I have ever seen." One mark was painted on the sheet and referred to the last year of Tutankhamen's reign. The other mark was woven by hand into the fabric and read: "Long live the Good King Nofer." Nofer was the name Smenkhkare assumed after Nefretete left Akhnaton.[6] "The signs are in white thread, the same

[6] Nofer-nofru-aten was the name adopted by Smenkhkare. Nefretete's full name was Nofer-nofru-Aten Nefretete.

155

color as the cloth itself, but, being a somewhat tighter weave, they are quite legible."

Among the pile of rags "three are of especial interest: these are kerchiefs." Such kerchiefs were worn by women over their hair, and Winlock, to illustrate this, inadvertently provided a photograph of a sculptured head of one of the princesses, daughters of Akhnaton, covered by a kerchief found by Davis. "All three had seen a good deal of use and had been washed so often that the edge had begun to come unsewed." "The two white ones have worn spots on the forehead." The third kerchief, a blue one, had been used "as some sort of scrubbing rag, so that it was worn all the way through in the middle." But originally these had not been rags: "All three kerchiefs are made of very light and fine linen."

Then there were many pots, smaller vessels and cups, too small to serve for more than one meal for one person. Seven vessels, of reddish-brown earthenware, have "labels written rapidly on them in hieratic from right to left in black ink": corn, *dsrt* (a drink), half loaf, grapes. There were also sixty-five identical cups, uninscribed, a wine jar, bottles, drinking vessels to hold water—"they appear to have sweated freely, the water leaving a thin film of mud in each." Among the objects were also four chips from a painted bowl and sixty-odd dishes of varying shape, size, and color. Many of the dishes had been broken and thrown into the larger jars.

"That we have here the remnants of a banquet is perfectly obvious from the bones which made up part of the contents of the jars." "The largest among the bones was a shoulder blade of a cow, hacked with some sort of heavy cleaver, and four ribs of a sheep or goat." The majority of the bones, however, make up parts of the skeletons of nine ducks belonging to at least three, and more probably four, different species of this animal, and bones of four geese, of three various species. All meat was cooked. There was no knife or fork or any sharp instrument, but "the Eighteenth Dynasty Egyptian did not use any sort of knife or fork but simply picked the food up in his hands to chew it."

In the pit were six or seven flower collars. "Some were torn by Mr. Davis to show how strong they still were." They were made of olive leaves, cornflowers, and berries of the woody nightshade. Were they worn by the participants of the banquet following the funeral of Tutankhamen? "None of them, however, was quite as elaborate as the collar found by Carter on the innermost coffin in the tomb of Tut-ankh-Amun, and we therefore assume that no one at this banquet had the rank of king."

Two brooms, "provided to sweep up sand or dust and to remove the last footprints of guests, were found in the jars. They are really nothing but fagots wrapped with a piece of cord around the middle." "Both brooms had seen hard use, perhaps sweeping away the footprints of those who attended the funeral ceremonies of King Tut-ankh-Amun."

Among the finds were a few lids of baked clay with a red slip. "A curious secondary use of all three of these lids was as lamps, for the inside of the smallest is thickly incrusted with black soot, and the other two contain what looks like the dried dregs of lamp oil, in one case flecked with soot. Since these are not real lamps, they could not have been used for the illumination of a palace hall."

And, finally, there was a small mask of a young woman made of plaster and painted. Such masks were made in the lifetime of a person usually of high standing or origin, and placed in his or her mortuary chamber. On this mask, which he reproduced, Winlock made only passing comment.[7]

Because of the presence of eight identical cups, Winlock decided that that many people partook of the funerary banquet.

[7] "It looks like a miniature mummy mask such as we would ordinarily expect to find on canopic bundles. . . ." Winlock.

He wrote: "It would be extremely interesting to know the names and quality of the persons who partook of this meal, but even in Egypt it would be asking a good deal to discover such details." Of course, if there was a banquet for Tutankhamen, King Ay would have been present—he officiated at the funeral—but not in the company of a few people, nor eating from earthen dishes. "It is enough to know that it was a meal which consisted of meat and fowl and probably bread and cakes. . . . At the end, as the eight people who partook of it withdrew from the room, their footprints were swept away and the door was closed." But Winlock admits that no other such cache of funerary banquets had ever been found, and probably had not been made: "I know of no other trace of gathering up of remains of such a meal."

Funerary banquets are known to have taken place in ancient Egypt, as pictures testify, but not from earthen dishes and certainly not from such ware in the case of the funerary banquet for Tutankhamen, when nothing other than golden vessels would have been used; and not by the light of a miserable sooty lamp made from an overturned lid, while in Tutankhamen's tomb beautiful alabaster lamps were stored; and sweeping away the footprints of the eight participants would not have worn down two brooms. How explain the odd number of various vessels besides the eight cups, such as sixty-five other cups, and the water jars that kept water for a long time, and the portions, such as a "half loaf" of bread? And the women's kerchiefs? The remains were not the remains of a royal embalming, and against this aspect of his idea, Winlock admits, speaks the fact that "we did not find, curiously enough, anything in the nature of a bed or platform on which the [royal] body could have been laid out," and the fine linen was not of the kind used in the embalming of a king, and the kerchiefs were meant to be worn in life.

The place, a cell seven by seven by six feet in the rocky floor of the Valley of the Kings,[8] was inhabited by a prisoner immured in it, who was supplied with food and other bare necessities. The prisoner was a woman, as the kerchiefs testify, of high origin, as the linen bears witness, linen even better than that used on the body of Tutankhamen. She spent a rather long time there, probably several months. The kerchiefs were worn where they had covered the brow and had been washed frequently—one of them had been used to scrub with, and natron was found there too. Water for drinking and washing and food were lowered in dishes and pots probably through an opening in the ceiling; when they were emptied, they were not removed but were replaced with others. The empty clay cups the prisoner put into jars that had contained water; the brooms were used much and were worn down; the earthenware lids were used to make a little light in the darkness of the cell at night, assuming that in the daytime there was a little of it from the opening in the ceiling.

The little female mask, the presence of which in the tomb-pit baffled its finders, could have been a part of the mortuary dowry of the young and noble person sentenced to a slow death "in the maiden's nuptial chamber, the caverned mansion of the bride of Death" (*Antigone*). It could be that whoever sentenced her to this cell, not wishing further to offend the gods, had given her in her prison tomb some of the things usually kept in readiness for the care of the dead.

The collars of flowers either were brought with the prisoner when she descended into the pit or were lowered to her by someone on the outside who still cared for her or even loved her; or, more probably, the prisoner herself wove these collars from field flowers and olive leaves thrown to her. The Greek legend has it that Haemon, the son of Creon, loved Antigone very dearly but was unable to save her.

[8] Winlock's measurements, 6½ by 4¼ by 7 feet, differ from Davis', given above.

Who, then, was this prisoner, immured only a minute's walk from the tomb of Tutankhamen and even closer to that of Smenkhkare? Who lived in the pit following the death of Tutankhamen and Smenkhkare? Who wove there into her tunic the words: Live, King Beautiful (Nofer)? Nofer was the fallen pretender.

She wove collars of field flowers, she swept her cell with the brooms until they were worn out, and she kept oil burning.

> Ah, fount of Dirce,
> and thou holy ground of Thebe
> whose chariots are many;
> Ye, at least, will bear me witness,
> in what sort, unwept by friends,
> and by what laws I pass
> to the rock-closed prison of my strange tomb,
> Ah me unhappy!
> Who has no home on the earth or in the shades,
> no home with the living or with the dead.[9]

[9] SOPHOCLES, *Antigone.*

"Only One Sister O'er His Bier"

"Only one sister o'er his bier
To raise a cry and pour the tear."
—AESCHYLUS

ONE minute's walk and we are again at the tomb that
concealed Smenkhkare's body. Fifty years after it was found
in 1907, the secret of "Tiy's tomb" still occupied the minds of
archaeologists and historians. In December of 1957 Sir Alan H.
Gardiner, the venerated Egyptologist, devoted a long article
to this tomb, conceding at its end that the facts are contra-
dictory and that the final solution must await some new
discovery.[1] But he established an important fact, namely, that
the love song at the feet of the deceased was written by a sister
of the dead man or by a wife who referred to him as her brother.
It was originally thought that the words were a prayer by the
dead person to the god; then, many years ago, it was found
that they were addressed by a female to the deceased. Gardiner
formulated it this way: "The first thing to be noticed is that
the woman whose name has been wilfully destroyed in line 1 of
the foot-end is presented not as the owner of the coffin, but
merely as a speaker." Then, examining the text and its erasures,

[1] Gardiner, "The So-called Tomb of Queen Tiye," *Journal of Egyptian
Archaeology*, XLIII (1957).

161

Gardiner finally established that the speaker referred to the dead man as her "brother"—the word was destroyed but could still be read; "brother" in a love song could stand for a husband or for the beloved. Gardiner's new rendering of the final lines is:

"Thou mayst call upon my name eternally, and it shall not fail from thy mouth, my beloved brother—thou being with me to all eternity. . . ."

Was it Nefretete addressing her beloved Akhnaton? Gardiner thought so at first, but before he finished his article he changed his mind and wrote: "It seems indispensable to believe that their [Akhnaton's and Smenkhkare's] intimacy was at Nefertiti's expense"; further, "Smenkhkare's nomen contains the epithet Nefernefruaten which had earlier belonged to Nefertiti." Nefretete would scarcely have written the song of love to Akhnaton in his grave. And, finally, it is "important to recognize that the possible allusion to Smenkhkare on the restored foot-end of the coffin has no bearing whatever upon the coffin's ownership." Smenkhkare was addressed in the love-prayer by a female and he was called there "brother"; the coffin, however, was Akhnaton's, the catafalque Tiy's.

In a long article in German, Günther Roeder brought together everything known or imagined about King Smenkhkare; he expressed his perplexity at the ill-assorted equipment in the tomb, "unworthy of a pharaoh," and his skepticism that this riddle would ever be solved. Roeder suggested that there must have been one faithful soul who had known the true religion of the dead king and placed a holy talisman with the name of Aton on his body: Smenkhkare had formally returned to the religion of Amon.[2]

Another important article concerning one of the finds in this tomb appeared recently in the *Bulletin* of the Metropolitan

[2] G. Roeder, "Thronfolger und König Smench-ka-Rê," *Zeitschrift für Aegyptische Sprache*, LXXXIII (1958), 43–74.

Museum of Art.[3] Cyril Aldred studied the hair styles of ancient Egypt and applied his knowledge to solve the problem of the identity of the portrait on the canopic jars found in Smenkhkare's tomb. The head on the lids of the canopic jars, one of which is in the Museum, is that of a female, one of the daughters of Akhnaton. At first the Museum labeled its jar as portraying Queen Tiy; when it was realized that the mummy was that of a male "the label of the Museum's specimen was altered to take these new theories into account" and the name of Akhnaton was written on it. Twenty years later "another change was made in the label, and this canopic jar lid was until very recently described as belonging to King Smenkhkare" because the mummy was recognized as his. Now it has a fourth label: the hair style is that of a female, and the head portrays a daughter of Akhnaton. Aldred concluded that the princess in question was the eldest daughter of Akhnaton and Smenkhkare's consort, Meritaten.

The erasures of the name on the jars were made by a careful hand, not with an intent to destroy, but only to obliterate, and all four heads were found intact. Thus it appears that the female who addressed the dead in her love song of parting gave him her own alabaster jars, carefully erasing her name from them, for they were to contain his viscera. It seems also that the princess used whatever pieces she could find for the clandestine burial. Meritaten, a half sister of Smenkhkare, was the historical Antigone, the authoress of the words of yearning at the feet of the dead whose body she washed and dressed and tended with drink-offering.

And who were the intruders who desecrated the place, made crude erasures, broke the catafalque, threw down the coffin, but left gold behind, even if they carried off some of the better pieces? "Many of the objects in the funerary equipment, includ-

[3] C. Aldred, "Hair Styles and History," *Metropolitan Museum of Art Bulletin*, XV (February 1957), 141–47.

ing the miniature canopic coffins, one of the enormous gold shrines, and some of the adornments which covered the mummy itself, had originally been made for Smenkhkare and were usurped for Tutankhamun's burial."[4] The intruders were emissaries of the new king, Ay, and they used the same seal—a jackal over nine prisoners—that appeared on the door of Tutankhamen's grave and the pit in the rock with the clay vessels in it.

Once more we turn the pages of Sophocles' *Antigone* and find that Creon sent emissaries to Polynices' grave. When Antigone was found over his body, "she cried aloud with the sharp cry of a bird in its bitterness, even as when, within the empty nest, it sees the bed stripped of its nestlings. So she also, when she saw the corpse bare, lifted up a voice of wailing, and called down curses on the doers of that deed . . . and from a shapely ewer of bronze, held high, with thrice-poured drink-offering she crowned the dead."[5] She saw the corpse denuded after she had already attended to it: the emissaries had undone what she had done before.[6] When convicted and sentenced by the king "to live a buried life," never again to see the "day-star's sacred eye," she spoke longingly of soon meeting her dead father, mother, and brother: "When ye died, with mine own hands I washed and dressed you, and poured drink-offerings at your graves; and now, Polyneices, 'tis for tending thy corpse that I win such recompense as this," namely, "tomb, bridal-chamber, eternal prison in the caverned rock."

The words about the sweet breath and the dear name of the fallen, written and secreted at the feet of her dead brother —Smenkhkare was her husband as well as brother—come once more to mind when we reread Euripides. His Antigone had

[4] Steindorff and Seele, *When Egypt Ruled the East*, p. 226. But cf. Roeder in the article referred to in Footnote 2.

[5] Sophocles, *Antigone*, trans. Jebb.

[6] Cf. Carl Robert, *Oidipus*, I, 369. "We bared the dank body well" (Messenger in *Antigone*).

not only the sisterly feeling of duty for the fallen brother Polynices, but she loved the dead dearly: "O my beloved! One kiss at least will I print upon thy lips." And again: "O my brother, Polyneices, name most dear to me!" In an ancient scholium Antigone was accused of having intimate relations with her brother.[7]

Creon, in condemning Antigone to a slow death, was also adamant in his resolve to desecrate the body of the fallen pretender and to leave it unburied. This was an unheard-of cruelty toward the dead and caused the intervention of the old seer Tiresias:

"Thou hast thrust children of the sunlight to the shades and ruthlessly lodged a living soul in the grave; but keepest in the world one who belongs to the gods infernal, a corpse unburied, unhonoured, all unhallowed." He warned that this was "a violence to gods" that would once more bring misery to the state, and already "the gods no more accept prayer and sacrifice at our hands."

Creon answered: "Old man, ye all shoot your shafts at me, as archers at the butts." He loudly voiced his suspicion that Tiresias was paid to make his plea. "Gain your gains, drive your trade, if ye list, in the silver-gold of Sardis and the gold of India; but ye shall not hide that man in the grave."

In the dialogue that followed, Creon again insulted the old seer: "The prophet-tribe was ever fond of money." The no less outspoken seer prophesied a dire future for the king: ". . . avenging destroyers lie in wait for thee . . . that thou mayest be taken in these same ills." His dead body one day would also be thrown out of his grave. "And mark well if I speak these things as a hireling."

Creon became troubled in his soul. The leader of the Chorus advised him: "Go thou, and free the maiden from her rocky chamber, and make a tomb for the unburied dead." He finally

[7] Marie Delcourt, *Oedipe* (1944), p. 219.

submitted and sent to the desecrated body, which had been left under guard, messengers who performed some pitiful semblance of funeral rites ("we washed the dead with holy washing").

Creon hurried to Antigone in her pit-tomb. But she was already dead, having ended her life, like her mother Jocasta, by her own hand. He found her "hanging by the neck, slung by a thread-wrought halter of fine linen" (Sophocles). One wonders about the long strips of fine linen torn from the sheet and missing in the pit-tomb in the Valley of the Kings, mentioned in Winlock's monograph.[8]

Like her mother Jocasta? Then how did Queen Tiy end her life?

[8] Winlock, *Materials Used at the Embalming of King Tut-ankh-Amun*, p. 8.

Tiy's End

O sun-god . . . how cursed
the beam thou didst
shed on Thebes. . . .
Jocasta, in *The Phoenissae* (Euripides)

TIY was at the height of her power and influence in the
twelfth year of Akhnaton's reign; then, as though a dark curtain
descended, the figure of the mother-wife could no longer be
discerned. Her end could be better understood if her mummy
were found in a royal tomb appropriate to her position during
her lifetime. But her mummy has not been found; her catafalque was broken; her son's coffin was found where hers should
have been; and in the coffin was the body of Smenkhkare.

Kurt Lange, in his book on Akhnaton,[1] places at the head
of "the series of problems not yet satisfactorily solved and
probably never to be solved" the question: Was the roughly
hewn rock cave prepared from the beginning as Queen Tiy's
last place of repose? For it speak the catafalque and other
funerary paraphernalia intended for her, and the site of the
cave, a short distance from the tomb of her parents. Against it
speak the humble appearance of the tomb and the meagerness
of the funerary equipment. Would the great royal wife of the
most lavish of the pharaohs of the glorious Eighteenth Dynasty,

[1] K. Lange, *König Echnaton und die Amarna-Zeit* (1951).

Amenhotep the Magnificent, who continued to wear the royal diadem in the days of their son Akhnaton, have been sent on her journey to the Great Beyond with less pomp than her parents and even her servants? How is it that the greatest queen Egypt ever knew was connected with that squalid tomb? Why was the queen so shabbily handled after her death? So asked historians.

And what happened to the body? Was her mummy transferred to the tomb of her husband, Amenhotep III? The supposed presence of Akhnaton's body in the same tomb would have been disgraceful because he was a heretic, and Tiy's mummy must have been carried away from his. So thought several scholars. But then it turned out not to be Akhnaton's body after all, and the theorizing grew more complicated and confused. Tiy's mummy was not found next to that of her husband, Amenhotep III, in the Valley of the Kings;[2] all that is left of her is a lock of hair found in the tomb of Tutankhamen with an ancient note identifying it as hers.

Then what was the end of the queen? In what adverse circumstances did she finish her life? Why was she treated as an outcast when her eyes closed? Why was her mummy removed even from the shabby tomb, as though the place was still too good for her?

Perhaps the Greek tradition can give us the answer to this strange state of affairs. Jocasta took her own life: Homer knew this, and the passage has been quoted on a previous page. Let us examine whether such an end for Tiy would explain many things left unexplained concerning her death.

All over the world, among the most disparate races, a suicide, unless he offers his life on the altar of his nation, is denied

[2] The mummy of Amenhotep III was found in the tomb of Amenhotep II, to which place the pious priests of the Twenty-first Dynasty transferred a number of royal mummies to save them from desecration by tomb robbers. In Professor Derry's opinion, however, the mummy ascribed to Amenhotep III is not his but that of a man of later date.

the honors that are due the dead. In some communities the suicide is buried outside the graveyard; in other places no funeral services are held and no cross or other marker is placed on his grave. His wandering spirit is feared. In all ancient societies, too, suicide was regarded as a sacrilege—unless it was committed as a religious self-sacrifice.

The Egyptians, for whom the concept of life after death was of eminent importance, must have been especially averse to giving funeral honors to a suicide. Thus it could have been for this reason that Tiy, if her end was like that of the legendary Jocasta, did not receive the appropriate honors due a queen. The mother-wife who hanged herself, though a queen and bearer of the royal diadem, deprived herself of the bliss of the life hereafter. No rich sepulcher would be erected for her, no libation for the subsistence of her spirit in the afterlife would be poured into her grave. Once more legend may explain what history has left as a riddle.

This may have been the secret of Tiy's end. She was not accorded a royal sepulcher, not even a sepulcher in any respect approaching the tombs excavated for the nobles of Thebes or el-Amarna; she was hidden away. If she took her own life she committed a grave sin in the sight of her people, the Egyptians.

But even from that humble place her body was removed, the catafalque enclosing her coffin was broken and damaged by erasures. For this desecration there was a reason too. The queen-mother lived in incest with her son. The name and the figure of her son-husband were chiseled away from the gold leaves of the catafalque, and the name of her first husband was written, instead, in ink. And this, also, is clear: the body of the widow who lived in incest with her son could not be put beside Amenhotep III. At the time of the restoration of Amon, Tiy's coffin was taken out of the catafalque and borne away from the secret burial place; its final destination is not known.

Thus the legend relating the story of Jocasta may explain

the strange facts of Tiy's burial. History, however, corrects the legend: Tiy would not have taken her life upon finding out that Akhnaton was her son; this she knew all along. Euripides, unlike Sophocles, lets Jocasta live until the tragic war between her two sons and then kill herself when she beholds their dead bodies.

If Tiy destroyed herself, it must have been in a fit of despondency. The gnawing knowledge of the sinfulness of her conduct may have played a role, though the origin of the incestuous relations with her son and the license for it were shown here to have sprung from Mitannian ethics. A decisive factor could have been the removal of Akhnaton from the throne or the proceedings that led to it, and the role Ay played against his sister in siding with his daughter. Depression in older people often follows humiliation or even a mere slight, whereas in younger people a nervous breakdown is more apt to occur when a person is confronted with a situation or a task that he or she feels incapable of handling.

Although the Egyptians placed much emphasis on the life hereafter, and suicide was a grave sin, the hidden urge to self-destruction, which, according to Freud, is ever present, along with the will to live, like the shadow of an illuminated object, was not unknown among the ancient worshipers of Osiris. In Egyptian literature the "Dialogue of the Tired of Life with His Soul" is one of the most beautiful and touching pieces of poetry. The soul tries to dissuade its bearer from his intent and reminds him that they will be denied the funeral rites. But the man answers:

> Behold, my name is detested,
> Behold, more than the smell of vultures
> on a summer's day when the sky is hot. . . .
> To whom can I speak today?
> Hearts are rapacious
> and there is no man's heart in which one can trust. . . .

To whom can I speak today?
The wrong which roams the earth,
there is no end to it. . . .
Death is in my sight today
as when a sick man becomes well,
like going out-of-doors after detention.
Death is in my sight today
like the smell of myrrh,
like sitting under an awning on a [breezy] day.
Death is in my sight today
like the perfume of lotuses,
like sitting on the shore of the Land of Drunkenness. . . .
Death is in my sight today
as when a man desires to see home
when he has spent many years in captivity.[3]

Even though in oriental communities, and in some occidental ones too, the body of the suicide is interred outside the hallowed ground of the communal cemetery, and his spirit is thought to walk at night, strangely enough, all over the world an object left by a suicide is looked upon as bringing good luck. It is a widely held belief that a piece of rope by which a person has hanged himself is a good-luck charm. In the grave of Tutankhamen a small box was found and in it was a lock of brown hair. A note identified the lock as having belonged to Queen Tiy.

Euripides had Jocasta cut her hair: ". . . I cut off my silvered locks and let them fall for grief with many a tear. . . ."

[3] Trans. R. O. Faulkner, in *Journal of Egyptian Archaeology*, XLII (1956).

"This Was Oedipus"

Now that the legends of the Thebaid cycle appear to have originated in historical events that took place in the palaces of Egypt, wonder may persist about certain clichés of mythological character interwoven in the story of Oedipus. He was exposed as a child, or doomed to die, threatened by a decree of a king, and so were Sargon I, king of Assyria, Moses, Jesus, even Judas Iscariot,[1] and a host of historical, semihistorical, and purely legendary characters. It may well be that the detail of the exposure of the infant Oedipus in the wasteland was but a legendary ornamentation and addition to the actual happenings that occurred to his historical prototype, and that all that took place following an inauspicious oracle was that the infant was sent away to relatives in a faraway region, instead of being exposed to die. This, however, cannot be asserted with certainty. The exposure motif could have been a true story: it is supported by the ever recurrent reference of the king to his having survived to live long. When Oedipus once more is supposed to lose his life following the disclosure of the oracle,

[1] According to a medieval legend preserved in a thirteenth-century manuscript, Judas Iscariot had a life story similar to Oedipus'. He was born on the island of Cariot (Crete), placed in a vessel on the seashore, was saved, killed his father, and married his mother. (Constans, *La Légende d'Oedipe*, pp. 95–103). If other parts of the legend are mythical, Crete as Judas' birthplace would have support from his name: Ish (man of) Cariot (Crete), a construction usual in biblical Hebrew.

expulsion again comes in lieu of death; a wanderer in the morning of his life, he is a wanderer in its evening too. "Sons and daughters of Thebes behold: this was Oedipus, greatest of men. . . . Behold, what a full tide of misfortune swept over his head."[2]

Another legendary cliché appears in the departure of a famous royal personage, at the sunset of his life, from his home into wandering and exile accompanied by a gentle and understanding daughter. Antigone, who went with her father into exile, giving up her own chance for a home and household, married life and children, created a prototype emulated by a daughter of another man prominent in his time, who, approaching the end of his life, was going into exile.

The present century has witnessed Leo Tolstoi who, one winter night left home and family and all that was dear and walked unobserved from the great estate of Yasnaya Polyana into a snowstorm. The devoted pupils of the Russian author and moralist, who taught simplicity but who lived in all the comfort of a country gentleman, had demanded of him that he show his dedication to his ideal of the life of a pauper, a wanderer of whom, according to the Gospel, the Lord takes care as He takes care of the birds of the field. Of all his children it was Alexandra who was taken into the plan, and she joined her father the day after his flight. Next, the entire world heard of Tolstoi's disappearance; then the news came that he had been found at a whistle stop ill with pneumonia. There he died, after several days of struggle with death, on November 8 (21), 1910, and was interred at Yasnaya Polyana without Christian rites. When Tolstoi was on his deathbed the Holy Synod of Russia decreed that no prayer should be said for the sick octogenarian; and when he died no requiem mass was permitted to be held for him in any Greek Orthodox church in Russia.[3]

[2] *Oedipus Rex*, trans. S. F. Watling.

[3] London *Times*, November 18 and 21–23, 1910.

In the present century, too, Anna was the one of Sigmund Freud's children who throughout his life was closest to him. She accompanied her father and mother into exile when Vienna was overrun by the Nazis. For many years Freud was sick, undergoing sixteen operations for cancer of the jaw; heroically he continued to work, to see patients and write books and articles, but he was tied to his home. In 1932 he wrote with a strong hand: "I would like to travel and nowhere more than to Palestine. But my invalid state permits me to carry on my life only at home." Yet in 1938 he went to the railway station in Vienna with his daughter Anna and made his way to England, where he died several months later.

Thus the legendary cliché about a famous man being accompanied in exile, like Oedipus, by a daughter has become historical truth, and more than once, in this century.

These daughters, who identified their spiritual life with that of their fathers, could be branded as suffering from an "Oedipus complex" or attachment above the filial, a term that, in psychoanalysis, is applied to a daughter as well as to a son.

Whoever has read the heartbreaking letters exchanged by Galileo and his daughter, a nun dying of tuberculosis in her cell, when he was forbidden to leave Florence for the remainder of his life and was losing his sight, he who had been first to see the mountains on the moon, the phases of Venus, and the satellites of Jupiter; or the description of the relation between John Milton's daughters and the poet, who as a young man visited the blind Galileo in Florence and then became blind too, and dependent on his daughters to whom he dictated his *Paradise Lost*—he knows that Antigone, who went into exile with her blind father, might have been more than a legendary figure.

Considering the entire scene at el-Amarna, it was most probably Beketaten who shared her father's exile, wandering, and humiliation. She was despised as the fruit of his union with his own mother. Thus, if a daughter accompanied Akhnaton in his exile, it could not be the same daughter who entombed her fallen brother and was immured in a pit tomb for having done so; the two roles of the legendary Antigone must have been performed by two different daughters of Akhnaton.

In Sophocles' version, the attribution of these two pious deeds (leading the blind father and burying the fallen brother) to one and the same person causes a difficulty and a complication in the plot of the plays. In *Oedipus Rex,* the play ends when Creon, deaf to Oedipus' plea, denies him the company of his daughters whom he leads away; but in *Oedipus at Colonus,* Antigone is with her father in exile and remains with him until his death. In *Antigone,* which takes place a few days later, no mention is made of her having wandered for years with her father.

Likewise, Euripides' Antigone has two roles that are incompatible. In the final scene of *The Phoenissae,* when, his two sons fallen, Oedipus is about to go into exile, Antigone insists that she will share her father's exile to the last, and at the same time she insists that she will bury her brother and accept death punishment for that. Obviously these two roles could not have been undertaken by one person.

The mortal remains of Akhnaton have never been found. In all probability the dead body of the exile was not mummified and is therefore not preserved; if he was given any tomb— except the unmarked grave of a wanderer—it is so well concealed that the place of his last repose is not known to man. The mausoleum he prepared for himself in the rock in the desert near Akhet-Aton when he was at the height of his power was not used. His sarcophagus was vengefully broken into bits. A wanderer in a strange land, or a stranger in his own land, he may have vainly longed for his members to be shrouded in the dust of his city.

"Will they shroud me in Theban dust?" was Oedipus' concern when he was on the throne. In Sophocles' version of the drama Oedipus decided to confer the blessing of his mortal remains on the people of Colonus, for wherever his body should lie, there would be favors from the gods and good fortune for the people of the land. Conscious of the value of his body, Oedipus, accursed in life, magnanimously decided to lie down in Colonus, thus blessing the entire land of Attica. In this village near Athens he died after he obtained the promise of Theseus, who pitied him, that the location of the tomb would remain unknown to men: this is the finale of *Oedipus at Colonus*. This drama, second in the sequence of the trilogy but the last to be written, was composed twenty-two years after Sophocles wrote *Oedipus Rex*, the first in historical sequence, and thirty-seven years after he wrote *Antigone*, the last part of the trilogy. When he was writing *Oedipus at Colonus*, Sophocles was nearing his ninetieth birthday and death. Although he wrote some one hundred and twenty plays, of which only seven are extant, his favorite hero occupied his mind before he died. Possibly he even felt some affinity between the unhappy "plaything of the gods" and himself; Sophocles chose Colonus for an obvious reason: this village was his own birthplace. I imagine also—and find that the same thought has already occurred to earlier scholars—that his son Iophon's accusation before the tribunal that he was incompetent to manage his affairs, as related by Cicero,[4] may have provided the emotional impetus for the powerful malediction that Oedipus, before his death, addressed to his elder son, who, fearing a military debacle, came to ask the blessing of his father's presence in his camp. That Sophocles identified himself in this last play with Oedipus can be seen also from the fact that he described Oedipus as very old, whereas in the play that serves as a sequel, but was written

[4] *De Senectute*, 22, R. C. Jebb rejects the story as spurious.

much earlier, Creon, Oedipus' uncle, is a vigorous middle-aged father of a young son.

Sophocles made the wanderer a source of blessing for the land in which he was to leave his mortal remains. This is in contrast to the old tradition that Oedipus could not find a town whose inhabitants would grant him a final resting place, and that even after his death his body was transferred from one place to another because everywhere people were afraid that a curse would be on the land that received the dead body of the unfortunate man who had risen so high and fallen so low. Finally he was hidden in a sacrarium of Demeter, whose oracle took pity on the unburied dead and forbade his removal, possibly because Demeter was the mother-goddess. Oedipus in death had to continue his wanderings, not unlike the dead Akhnaton, according to the assumption of those who have studied the royal graves of el-Amarna and Thebes.

Sophocles left Oedipus with no hope in this world but in some "mysterious communion with unseen powers." Thus he changed the curse into a blessing and placed his own benediction on his martyred hero before departing himself for Hades.

Until now we have omitted to examine one detail, namely, the length of Akhnaton's reign as compared with the number of years accorded to Oedipus on the throne. Akhnaton reigned sixteen years, the seventeenth being the latest to which any inscription testifies. "Year 17 still remains the highest recorded date of Akhenaten's reign."[5] Yet some scholars took the view that he ruled twenty years, the twenty-first being his last.[6]

What does the Greek legend have to say about the length of Oedipus' reign? "Teiresias comes to the king to tell the secret

[5] H. W. Fairman in Frankfort and Pendlebury, *The City of Akhenaten*, Part II (1933), p. 103.

[6] K. C. Seele, *Journal of Near Eastern Studies*, XIV (1955), 175.

which he has kept for sixteen years."[7] But a longer reign is also ascribed to Oedipus: "Twenty years have passed since then. A pestilence falls upon the city."[8]

To both Akhnaton and Oedipus are ascribed reigns of sixteen and of twenty years. It is possible that the latter figure includes the years when Akhnaton was still in his capital, though no longer the actual ruler, a semiprisoner in the palace. Desroches-Noblecourt actually refers to Akhnaton as living in exile in the south of his capital.[9]

As to the length of his elder son's reign, Smenkhkare-Polynices reigned one year only. Both the Greek legend and history are in agreement on this point. Although the last date of Smenkhkare's reign is year "third," Roeder in his recent article on Smenkhkare states: "The duration of his reign was not three calendar years, but only a little more than one single year."[10] The younger brother did not vacate the throne when his year's reign was over and it was years before the elder was able to return with his allied armies and attempt to regain the crown. Tutankhamen's last year was the eighth, but it is probable that his count started with the seventeenth year of Akhnaton's reign and does not recognize Akhnaton's last years and the reign of Smenkhkare.

It is the prevailing view that Akhnaton mounted the throne at the age of twenty-four or twenty-five, or a few years later, and left it when he was in his forties.[11]

[7] Gilbert Murray, *A History of Ancient Greek Literature* (1907), p. 240.

[8] E. Capps, *From Homer to Theocritus* (1901), p. 226.

[9] Ch. Desroches-Noblecourt in Schaeffer, *Ugaritica III*, p. 194.

[10] Roeder, "Thronfolger und König Smench-ka-Rê," *Zeitschrift für Aegyptische Sprache*, LXXXIII (1958) Heft I, 45.

[11] Seele, *Journal of Near Eastern Studies*, XIV (1955), considers that Akhnaton ended his reign at the age of forty-seven, after twenty-one years on the throne.

It has often been surmised that the brothers Smenkhkare and Tutankhamen were sons of Tiy and Amenhotep III. However, it has also been pointed out that they could not have been sons of Amenhotep III: Tutankhamen died at the age of seventeen or eighteen after his own reign of seven years (Smenkhkare's one-year reign having been ascribed to Tutankhamen) and sixteen or seventeen years of Akhnaton's reign. Similarly Smenkhkare, who died at the age of twenty-three at the same time as Tutankhamen, must have been a son of Akhnaton. Carter wrote of these two princes as sons of Akhnaton. Roeder, in his work on Smenkhkare, is not averse to ascribing Smenkhkare's and Tutankhamen's parentage to Akhnaton,[12] agreeing with the verdict of Professor Derry, the anatomist. Thus not Amenhotep III but Akhnaton was the father of these two princes. Their mother still could have been Tiy.

[12] Roeder, *Zeitschrift für Aegyptische Sprache*, LXXXIII (1958), Heft I, 45, 72. Carter, *The Tomb of Tut-ankh-Amen*, III, 18.

King Ay and a "Tumult of Hatred"

AT AN advanced age Ay became king in Thebes. So that he might occupy the throne, he had had both young kings removed, one after the other. First, Smenkhkare was deposed through the stratagem of a temporary cession in favor of his brother. Then Tutankhamen was encouraged to meet his rival-brother in combat. No one who cared for the seventeen- or eighteen-year-old king would have sent him to the front lines, or even into a duel, but it served Ay's purpose perfectly.

The succession of kings in Egypt was through the female line. Amenhotep III broke with this tradition by marrying Tiy, who was not a royal princess. However, Amenhotep III was himself of royal blood, whereas Ay was not and could not claim origin from Ra. He was concerned with this problem and he solved it. Tutankhamen died childless, after his wife had borne him two stillborn children, both found mummified in his tomb. Ay, in order to establish his own right to the throne, married Tutankhamen's widow, the sixteen-year-old Ankhesenpaaten, now renamed Ankhesenamen, his own granddaughter.[1] Soon one hears no more of Ankhesenamen.[2]

[1] P. E. Newberry, "King Ay, the Successor of Tut-ankh-amun," *Journal of Egyptian Archaeology,* XVIII (1932), 50–52.

[2] On the ground of cuneiform documents found in Boghazkoi in Asia Minor an assumption has been made repeatedly that the widowed Ankhesenamen wrote to a Hittite king, asking him for a son to become

Euripides has Creon, too, claim his right to the vacant throne not by virtue of his being a brother-in-law of the king, but through a daughter of Oedipus whom he planned to marry to his son. Creon said to the dethroned Oedipus: "Eteocles, thy son, left me to rule this land, by assigning it as a marriage portion to Haemon with the hand of thy daughter Antigone." This succession to the throne through the female line was Egyptian and characteristic of the Eighteenth Dynasty.

Whereas Akhnaton when on the throne assumed the appellation "Who liveth in truth," Ay, upon becoming king, applied to himself the cognomen, "Who is doing right." Such titles were rather unusual among the kings of Egypt. Yet one may understand Ay's selecting this motto. Like Creon of the Oedipus cycle, Ay professed to be doing his duty to the crown and the nation by deposing Akhnaton, installing Akhnaton's sons, and then siding with the younger son in the brothers' conflict.

Ay's cruelty against Meritaten was also dictated by his desire to preclude the appearance of some other pretender who, by marrying Smenkhkare's widow, the eldest daughter of Akhnaton, would acquire equal or better rights to the crown than he himself. Besides, Ay could not forgive Meritaten for siding against Nefretete, her mother and his daughter.

Nefretete was a daughter of his by an early marriage; his first wife died, as Aldred demonstrated and earlier scholars conjectured, and Nefretete was nursed and brought up by Ty, his second wife. Therefore Ty had the title "Queen's nurse,"[3] and in the unfinished sepulcher at Akhet-Aton she is pictured near her husband before the royal pair and described in writing as "Queen's nurse."

---

her husband. In the final volume of *Ages in Chaos* I shall identify the Egyptian queen-widow, named in cuneiform Dahamun, as Dakh-hat-amun of a later dynasty.

[3] Weigall, *The Life and Times of Akhnaton*; Aldred, *Journal of Egyptian Archaeology*, XLIII (1957).

Ay's second wife and later his queen, Ty, had the same name as Queen Tiy, Ay's sister; it is only for the purpose of differentiation that their names are spelled differently in English.

Euripides has a son of Creon say to his father: "I will [go] to thy sister, Jocasta, at whose breast I was suckled as a babe when reft of my mother and left a lonely orphan. . . ."[4] In history, as in the legend, Creon-Ay's first wife died young, probably in childbirth.[5]

History has it that Ay married a namesake of his sister, the queen, and that this second wife nursed and brought up the orphan; in the legend it was the queen herself who nursed her brother's orphans. The strangeness of the legend of a queen serving as a nurse for children not her own is resolved by the historical fact that Queen Tiy and Ay's wife Ty had identical names.

After Ay buried Tutankhamen he completed the building of a much larger sepulcher for himself. Tutankhamen's tomb had originally been built for Ay by his brother-in-law, Amenhotep III, not far from the tomb of his parents, Yuya and Tuya, in the Valley of the Kings. For Tutankhamen, when he mounted the throne, a tomb was being prepared close to that of Amenhotep III; it is probable that it was first planned for Smenkhkare, when he occupied the throne; but neither of the brothers was entombed in it. Ay finished the royal tomb for himself. He intended to have his last abode in this rich mausoleum. The walls of his royal tomb were adorned with decorations and colored scenes, and Ay prepared for himself a sarcophagus as precious as that in which he entombed Tutankhamen. The abandoned sepulchral chamber in Akhet-Aton, the heretical residence, was never finished; it became a place for jackals and owls.

[4] Euripides, *The Phoenissae*, trans. E. P. Coleridge.

[5] Aldred, in the article referred to above, assumes that Ay's first wife died in childbirth and his second wife nursed Nefretete.

Very little is known of Ay's reign; yet it is known that the old king, who reigned only a short time, did not close his eyes in peace. "Anarchy ensued. Thebes was a prey of plundering bands who forced their way into the royal tombs."[6] The invaders found the greatest satisfaction in demolishing Ay's tomb, his place of repose being selected for the most thorough destruction. The rich sarcophagus was broken into small fragments. The pictures and inscriptions cut in the walls were defaced. It was not a case of mere tomb robbery: it was an act of violence and vengeance.

The prophecy of the blind seer was fulfilled. In *Antigone* he prophesied that Creon, too, would be dishonored after his death and thrown out of his tomb. The condition of Ay's sepulcher shows that this really happened. "His sarcophagus was broken to pieces and, apparently, his body was destroyed."[7]

For the "violence done to gods infernal" in denying burial to an unhonored and unhallowed corpse, "a time not long to be delayed shall awaken the wailing of men and women in thy house. And a tumult of hatred against thee stirs all cities. . . ."

We may figure out who the avengers were: these were the Epigoni. In Greek tradition, the Seven against Thebes and their armies were repelled, but after ten years their sons, the Epigoni, returned and ravished Thebes. From whence came the foreign bands, first called by Smenkhkare to help him to regain the throne, will be disclosed in the light of the history of the period that followed the close of the Eighteenth Dynasty, in the work dedicated to a reconstruction of history.

[6] Breasted, *A History of Egypt*, p. 394.

[7] G. Steindorff, "Die Grabkammer des Tutanchamun," *Annales du Services des Antiquités de l'Egypte*, XXXVIII (1938), 667.

The Curse

In all places at all times civilized nations have cared for the disposal of the bodies of their dead, but neither in Judea nor in Assyria, Chaldea, Greece, or Rome was there such a cult of the dead as there was in Egypt, nor was such importance attached to the care of the dead by the living. The belief in the afterlife, in which the body participates, caused Egyptians, even those of modest means, to mummify their dead and to supply them with all the necessities of life, including a dwelling. Some other peoples, notably the Carians, also built expensive burial chambers and offered libations to the deceased, but nowhere were the cult of the dead and the care of the living for their places of entombment of such interest to kings and ordinary mortals as in Egypt. The tombs of Thebes and of el-Amarna with their wall decorations bear witness to this all-important subject in the life of the Egyptians.

Since antiquity treasure-hunting violators looking for gold, jewels, and furniture have robbed the tombs of their riches and desecrated the mummies. "He [the god] shall deliver them into the flaming wrath of the king on the day of his anger; his serpent-diadem shall spit fire upon their heads, shall consume their limbs, shall devour their bodies. . . . They shall be engulfed in the sea, it shall hide their corpses. They shall not receive the mortuary ceremonies of the righteous. . . . Their sons shall not be put into their places, their wives shall be violated while their eyes see it. . . . They shall belong to the sword on the day of destruction . . . they shall hunger, without bread, and their bodies shall die."

So wrote Amenhotep, son of Hapu, on the wall of his mortuary temple built in the western plain of Thebes, among the mortuary temples of the kings, and he aimed his words against violators of his temple whether motivated by greed or by politics. An echo of this vehement language is heard in the speech Sophocles put in the mouth of Tiresias when he cursed Creon for denying burial to the fallen prince.

The Egyptian origin of the Theban cycle of legends can be recognized in the fact that the question of burial is so much in the forefront of the plot. The theme of *Oedipus at Colonus* and, to an equal degree, of *Antigone* and *Seven against Thebes* is the problem of burial. The great concern of Oedipus when he was king was to be buried in Theban soil after his death, but after his exile he would not return to Thebes to have his remains buried there. In Sophocles' version of the legend, he insisted that his grave be hidden and its site remain unknown to all except the king of the land of Attica, in a manner not unknown in Egypt, where kings concealed their tombs.

For attacking Thebes in his effort to regain the throne, Polynices, by decree of the regent of the kingdom, is denied burial, while Eteocles, his rival, is given a sumptuous burial with all rites. This alone would be natural in any setting, Greek or otherwise,[1] but Antigone's long monologue in which she bewails her dead brother's doom—not his death—is without parallel in the entire Greek literature.

This preoccupation with burial and the supreme importance attached to the last resting place are Egyptian in character, not Greek.

[1] Cf. the final scene of *Ajax* by Sophocles.

Antigone's "caverned pit-tomb in the rock" is not Greek either. The Greeks sometimes cremated their dead, at others entombed them in the earth, but only very rarely they cut into rock to make a tomb. The Egyptians, however, at Thebes and at el-Amarna, did cut their tombs in rock. Thus a tomb in caverned rock was foreign to the Greeks.

The burial rags of Smenkhkare in a coffin not his own; the golden shrines and coffins of Tutankhamen; Ay's demolished and desecrated sepulcher; the secreted corpse of the king's mother and wife; the death chamber of a young and noble prisoner—all these sepulchers, tombs, and hiding places in the Valley of the Kings at Thebes live in the supplications of Oedipus at Colonus, in the edict of Creon, in the wailing dirges of Antigone.

For the very reason that the tomb and the afterlife connected with it were of such significance for an Egyptian, the mummy and its tomb were subject to desecration and destruction by the enemies of the dead. He could be punished more effectively after his death than before; he could be made "a nameless outcast, wandering unrecognized and unpitied through the vast underworld."[2] This was the reason for the orgy of destruction in the tombs of el-Amarna and Thebes. To protect a tomb from desecration by political foes or treasure hunters (ancient prototypes of modern safecrackers), there were only two things the Egyptian kings and nobles could do: hide their tombs and invoke a curse against violators. The ancients believed in the efficacy of the curse and the belief is as long-lived as the belief in benediction.

In modern times this belief in the curse has never been so widespread as when Lord Carnarvon died five months after the discovery of the tomb of Tutankhamen, before the inner shrine, sarcophagus, and coffins were opened. He died of blood poison-

[2] A. Weigall, *The Life and Times of Akhnaton*, p. 242.

ing, presumably following a mosquito bite, which was rumored to have become infected when he handled some poisonous fabric or vessel. Protective curses on the shrines were blamed for his death. An evil omen was recalled. Arthur Weigall, who at the time of the discovery of the tomb was inspector general in charge of antiquities in Egypt, gave this account:

"During the recent excavations which led to the discovery of the tomb of Tutankhamen, Mr. Howard Carter [the discoverer] had in his house a canary which daily regaled him with its happy song. On the day, however, on which the entrance to the tomb was laid bare, a cobra entered the house, pounced on the bird, and swallowed it. Now, cobras are rare in Egypt, and are seldom seen in winter; but in ancient times they were regarded as the symbol of royalty, and each Pharaoh wore the symbol upon his forehead, as though to signify his power to strike and sting his enemies." Those who believed in omens, therefore, interpreted the incident as meaning that the spirit of the new-found pharaoh was warning the intruders. "At the end of the season's work, Lord Carnarvon was stung mysteriously upon the face, and died. Millions of people throughout the world have asked themselves whether the death of the excavator of this tomb was due to some malevolent influence which came from it."[3]

These occurrences were all coincidental, but they seem even stranger now that we know that the tomb was occupied by the last king of the house of Laius, which was indeed rich in curses. It was almost as though the last act of the Theban trilogy had never been played until recent times.

[3] A. Weigall, *Tutankhamen and Other Essays* (1923), p. 110.

Trails Over the Sea

When, shortly before the Trojan War, kings ruled in Mycenae in the Argive plain, there were commerce and traffic between Greece and Egypt. In the Thebes of Amenhotep III and in the el-Amarna of Akhnaton, Mycenaean ware has been found in large quantities; and in Mycenae and the neighboring Tiryns objects from the Egypt of Amenhotep III have been uncovered.[1] A scarab, or signet, bearing the name of Queen Tiy was found in Mycenae; and it has been observed that it is from this time on that Egyptian objects appear in continental Greece. Even exact reproductions of decorations on the ceilings of the tombs in Egyptian Thebes were discovered in the tombs of Mycenae and Orchomenos.[2]

As for Thebes in Boeotia, "there is no historical record of any traffic between [it] and Egypt. Indeed there is no place in which it would be more unlikely to find any trace of such."[3] Yet one object of Egyptian origin was found in Boeotia: a scarab with a winged sphinx engraved on it. "This one object is obviously a 'souvenir' of some wandering adventurer," wrote

[1] J. D. S. Pendlebury, *Aegyptiaca, a catalogue of Egyptian objects in the Aegean area* (1930).

[2] Breasted, *A History of Egypt*, p. 388.

[3] Pendlebury, *Aegyptiaca*, p. 87.

J. D. S. Pendlebury in his catalogue of Egyptian objects found in Greece and on the Aegean islands. In Athens in Attica, several Egyptian objects have been found. "The only Egyptian objects found in Athens antedate by far our knowledge of any historical connections." Here, too, Pendlebury assumed the arrival of some wandering adventurer. Single adventurers in Boeotia and Attica, but regular traffic between Mycenae and Egypt in the same age—and how far is it from Mycenae to Athens? Only fifty-five miles as the crow flies. If a signet of Queen Tiy reached Mycenae, her story would have reached it too, and the neighboring cities as well.

As we have already said, the city on the Nile had been known to the Greeks by the name of Thebes since the time of Homer; the Egyptian name for it was No (the residence) or No-Amon. Then why did the Greeks call the city in Egypt by the name of the city in Boeotia? Or if, conversely, the Greeks first called the Egyptian city by that name and later transferred the name to the city in Boeotia, what was the reason for this?

Was the story of the royal house of No in Egypt transplanted and attached to Thebes in Boeotia because of the identity of the names of these cities? Or was one of the cities subsequently called by the name of the other for the very reason of the story and the place of its real happening?

A wandering adventurer or bard could have brought the story to Thebes or to Athens—it is not necessary that the story should first have been a Theban saga, which Athens later obtained from there.[4] Several centuries passed and the great tragedians of Athens—Aeschylus, Sophocles, and Euripides—wrote trilogies on the subject of the incestuous king and his house. The place of action was planted in Thebes in Boeotia. There, however, no monument or grave remained to testify to the story. It

[4] "The occurrence of greatest moment for European literature was the penetration of the Oidipous-legend and cult into Attica." L. R. Farnell, *Greek Hero Cults and Ideas of Immortality* (1921), p. 333.

may have been that Thebes was made the scene of the happenings in order to stigmatize that city, which was often in conflict with other Greek cities. Or possibly Cadmus, the founder of the Boeotian city, who came from Phoenicia, was a contemporary of the events described in this book; elsewhere I have intimated that he may have been King Nikmed of Ugarit, who lived in the days of the el-Amarna correspondence, applied cuneiform to the Hebrew alphabet, made of cuneiform an alphabetic writing, and, together with the Ionians, was expelled from his city by Assyrian conquerors and fled by sea.[5] Cadmus introduced the Hebrew alphabet into Greece and applied it to the Greek language. King Nikmed had an Egyptian princess as his wife;[6] and the legend has it that Cadmus brought with him a wife named Sphinx.[7] Thebes in Egypt was, in Nikmed's day, the greatest city in the world; the tragedy of its royal house could not have remained secret or have failed to make a strong impression in neighboring Phoenicia; and the Greeks, expelled from Ugarit together with Nikmed, founders of the Cadmean Thebes, could have been the first narrators of the terrible events that shook Egypt and its dependencies. Euripides' extant tragedy about the Theban royal house is named *The Phoenissae* because of the chorus of Phoenician women who speak revealingly to the heroes of the play—and to the playgoers; why a Phoenician chorus in a Greek tragedy?

It is also probable that the story reached the shores of Greece through more than one channel.

In one sentence Sophocles expressed himself as though he knew the actual place of the happenings. Speaking of his sons, Polynices and Eteocles, Oedipus exclaims: "O, true image of

[5] *Ages in Chaos*, I, "The End of Ugarit," 219ff.

[6] Ch. Desroches-Noblecourt, in Schaeffer, *Ugaritica III*, 219, n. 2; Schaeffer, in *Syria*, XXXI (1954), 56, Plate 9.

[7] Pauly-Wissowa, *Real-Encyclopädie*, Second Series, Vol. III, Col. 1724.

the ways of Egypt that they show in their spirit and their life!"
(*Oedipus at Colonus.*) But the words that follow nullify the
impression.[8] However, Sophocles twice refers to Thebes as the
city "of many chariots." Antigone implores: "Ah, fount of Dirce,
and thou holy ground of Thebe whose chariots are many; Ye,
at least, will bear me witness. . . ." The fount of Dirce was in
Boeotian Thebes. But the appellation "Thebes of many chariots" (*Antigone*, line 149) must have been associated in the Greek
mind with the Egyptian Thebes: in Homer, Achilles speaks of
the hundred-gated Thebes as a city of many chariots, two
hundred to each gate.[9]

In Euripides, one of the gates where the combats of the Seven
against Thebes took place is called the Ogygian port (gate).[10]
The time of Ogygus was much earlier than that of Cadmus and
the foundation of the city. And scholars think that this gate,
though named as the chief among the city gates, was an invention of the creator of the Theban epic.[11] On the other hand,
Aeschylus calls the city in Egypt "the Ogygian Thebes."[12]
These instances, and a few others, create the impression that
the Greek tragedians of the fifth century were not entirely ignorant of the place of the real happenings. My impression may
be erroneous and Sophocles and Euripides may have known
no more than did Aeschylus where the events actually took
place. Yet if they did not know it, the epic story told by one
bard to another, the very source from which the tragedians borrowed, contained a few elements that betray the secret of the
land of the historical happenings.

[8] "For there the men sit weaving in the house, but the wives go forth
to win the daily bread." Sophocles borrowed the sentence from Herodotus,
his contemporary (Herodotus, II, 35).

[9] *Iliad*, IX, 383f.

[10] *The Phoenissae*, l. 1113.

[11] Von Wilamowitz in *Hermes*, XXVI (1891), 216–17, 241.

[12] Aeschylus, *The Persians*, 37.

W. E. Gladstone is remembered as Queen Victoria's great Prime Minister, who dedicated his life to politics and debates in the House of Commons, repeatedly taking over the helm of the ship of state. Not so well known, however, is the fact that he spared some of his time for the study of Homer, a subject on which he wrote several volumes and lectured at Oxford, even after reaching the age of eighty, so sustained was his interest in Homer. In his *Homeric Synchronisms: an Enquiry into the Time and Place of Homer* (1876), he developed the thesis that many of the Greek legendary motifs originated in oriental countries and more especially in Egypt. Gladstone wrote: "I had been struck by the predominance of a foreign character and associations in the Homeric Underworld of the Eleventh Odyssey," populated by people of Phoenician and other non-Hellenic origin, among which he also counted the Cadmeian seer Tiresias, whereas "the recent Hellenic Dead, furnished by the [Trojan] war, are wanderers in the Shades, without fixed doom or occupation, scarcely, as it were, naturalised in their new abode."[13]

Homer looked on Egypt as the land of knowledge, including hermetic, or secret and mysterious, knowledge. He has Menelaus travel to Egypt in order to learn about the future and about the existence of the Elysian fields.[14] "The references in the poems to Egyptian Thebes prove that they belong to the period when the city was supreme in Egypt, and was in effect the first city of the known world." Achilles, in stating that no riches could induce him to comply with Agamemnon's wish, spoke of the wealth of Thebes in Egypt, "the city which contained the greatest treasures in the world." Homer represented Thebes as possessing twenty thousand chariots drawn by horses (more than all the taxicabs in the five boroughs of New York).

[13] P. 213.

[14] Ibid., p. 233.

Homer was never in Egypt. "The Poet must have been in the way of gathering all the whispers wafted from the East and South, whether by seamen, by immigrants, or by official representatives of the great Empire and their naturalised descendants."[15]

Yet Gladstone did not think, in this connection, of the Theban cycle of legends and of the Oedipus drama; he scrutinized many legendary heroes, but the name of Oedipus and his wife and children are not even mentioned in the book. He apparently thought of them as Greek.

The transformation the events underwent in crossing the Mediterranean and acquiring the guise of a legend was accompanied by the introduction of a new, characteristically Hellenic element. The Greeks believed in fate; for them the future was predestined, and if the gods decreed doom for a man and his house, nothing could be done to change it. Whatever a person did, however much he tried to elude the dire future, his doom would find him out. The future was known to the gods, and it could be made known to mortals with the help of an oracle or a medium employed at the sanctuary of a god.

Before Oedipus was born he was doomed. Whatever his parents did, whatever he did, events only brought him ever closer to the lot preordained for him. Of no avail were supplications to the gods, pious deeds, or fasting and the putting on of sackcloth; they were not even tried by the doomed. "But dreadful is the mysterious power of fate; there is no deliverance from it by wealth or by war, by fenced city, or dark, sea-beaten ships." (Chorus, *Antigone*.)

This fatalism is essentially a Greek concept. It was not conducive to good deeds, to reconsideration of ways of life and to mending them. What could Oedipus have done, and did not, to avoid the horror that awaited him from a time before he

15 Ibid., p. 272.

was born? But the ethical motive is not entirely lacking: Laius was doomed to be killed by his son for having been the first to introduce unnatural love on Greek soil.

Thus a crime for which retribution is exacted is present, but no good deed on the part of the sinner can atone for the crime; the son of the guilty must suffer for his father's misdeed not only by becoming a parricide but also by committing another crime for which he and his children after him will suffer to the last.

In agony the condemned cries out, "I wail in the stress of my terror, and shrill in my cry of despair," but there is no pity among the gods; and the doomed man has no choice but to acquiesce in what has been ordained. "Why should we fawn and flinch away from doom?"[16]

Oedipus suffered for the crime of his father and for no crime of his own; and Oedipus' children were also born for punishment.

> The sacred seed-plot, his own mother's womb,
> he sowed, his house's doom,
> a root of blood!

In the fate of Oedipus' children the moral link is once more forged between the crime and the punishment. Actually there are two links: the princes killed each other because this had been a part of the doom of the house of Oedipus, and they suffered because of the curse which their father placed upon them for having expelled him, a blind king, from his house and his kingdom. Thus their ancestral doom was sealed before they were born, and the paternal curse pursued them, too, for their own deeds. Yet it was the first that was in some way the cause of the latter. Said Eteocles: "The god is urgent for our doom."

The son of a sinner is doomed not only to suffer but to commit

[16] Aeschylus, *The Seven Against Thebes.*

a sin of his own, and if he is virtuous by nature he is compelled to such an action in ignorance of what he is doing. The Greek hero killed a wayfarer, which, it appears, by Greek standards, was no crime, especially as he was provoked to his action and did not know whom he killed. He married his mother and did not know who she was. In presenting the incest as a crime of which the participants were unaware, Greek poets again intensified the drama; for them the very idea of a fate that could not be escaped was the most tragic element in the development of the events. The innocence of the victims made the Hellenes feel more strongly the growing terror of an impending doom; and their sympathy was intensified because the innocent neither intended their crimes nor were conscious of committing them. In this the Christian feeling about suffering accords with the Hellenic feeling for tragedy, and stories of innocent martyrs crucified, immured, or made a target for arrows occupy an important place in patristic literature. Modern man, however, derives much more pleasure from the story of an innocent person who first suffers under suspicion of being the perpetrator of a crime and then is absolved when the real evildoer is tracked down and killed or otherwise punished, and it is on this formula that the entire literature of crime and its detection has grown.

The Seer of Our Time

I F T H E *Oedipus Rex* is capable of moving a modern reader or playgoer no less powerfully than it moved the contemporary Greeks, the only possible explanation is that . . . there must be a voice within us which is prepared to acknowledge the compelling power of fate in the *Oedipus*. . . . His fate moves us only because it might have been our own, because the oracle laid upon us before our birth the very curse which rested upon him. It may be that we were all destined to direct our first sexual impulses toward our mothers, and our first impulses of hatred and violence toward our fathers; our dreams convince us that we were. King Oedipus, who slew his father Laius and wedded his mother Jocasta, is nothing more or less than a wish-fulfilment—the fulfilment of the wish of our childhood."[1]

So wrote Sigmund Freud in his most important and most renowned book, *The Interpretation of Dreams*. The passage quoted is probably the most noteworthy in that book, and Freud himself added to it in later editions: "None of the discoveries of psychoanalytical research has evoked such embittered contradiction, such furious opposition, and also such entertaining acrobatics of criticism, as this indication of the incestuous impulses of childhood which survive in the unconscious."

[1] *The Basic Writings of Sigmund Freud* (Modern Library, 1938), trans. Dr. A. A. Brill, p. 308.

If there is truth in our thesis that the legend of Oedipus grew from the real experiences of the Pharaoh Akhnaton and his family, then Freud erred in assuming that no historical substratum, but only a hidden urge common to all of us, is the source from which sprang the plot of the ancient legend. Nevertheless, as pointed out in the beginning of this discourse, the hold exerted on our imagination by the legend of King Oedipus can be explained by the echo it awakens in the dark recesses in the minds of so many of us, independent of the fact that Oedipus is himself a mirror image of a historical personality.

Freud did not realize that his two heroes—Oedipus, of his first book, and Akhnaton, of his last book[2]—were one person. In recognizing the Oedipus mechanism or complex in man, ancient and modern, Freud showed an insight that made him the slayer of the monster hidden in our unconscious minds, and thus a patron-healer of all the maladjusted. Freud was predestined to make this discovery concerning the structure of human character at an age when he still walked on all fours. His mother was young, the second wife of his father, who at the time of Sigmund's birth was already a grandfather; Sigmund had a nephew, a playmate, older than himself. His mother was very much attached to him and he remained strongly attached to her even when he was in his seventies and she in her nineties; but, as he himself wrote, the grown-up man is continuously attached to the image of his mother as he knew her when he was a child and she was young. Toward his father Sigmund had ambivalent feelings, jealousy and hatred dominating over attachment and affection. When his father died and Freud was in his early forties, a tide of creativeness was liberated in him, and he wrote *The Interpretation of Dreams*. One would certainly assume that Freud, who recognized the prevalent role of the Oedipus complex, also overcame it: the recognition of a complex is almost

[2] *Moses and Monotheism.*

197

tantamount to conquering it. Yet Sigmund Freud's was a different case, and of this he himself gave proof in his last book, *Moses and Monotheism*, written at the age of eighty and published shortly before his death. In that book Freud tried to prove that Moses was but a disciple of Akhnaton, the first monotheist; Akhnaton was "the first and perhaps the purest case of monotheistic religion in the history of humanity."

One is surprised to read this evaluation of Akhnaton by the author of *The Future of an Illusion*, in which Freud described religion—all religion—as a kind of neurosis of fear and compulsion. He omitted to use the scalpel of psychoanalysis on Akhnaton. He also failed to realize that sun worship cannot be termed monotheism, but only monolatry. And unless his inner motives are understood, one is equally baffled by Freud's insistence on writing and publishing as his last book—almost as his last testament—his degradation of Moses. He degraded him by denying him originality; simultaneously he degraded the Jewish people by denying them a leader of their own race, for he made Moses an Egyptian; and finally he degraded the Jewish God, making of Yahweh a local deity, an evil spirit of Mount Sinai. On the eve of his departure from a long life he had to blast the Hebrew God, demote his prophet, and glorify an Egyptian apostate as the founder of a great religion. Freud admitted that he had to overcome an inner difficulty in deciding to publish his *Moses and Monotheism* at a time when Hitler had already made known his plan to decimate, even to annihilate, Freud's own race. But he felt compelled to do so because he, like Akhnaton, was dedicated to "living in truth." He could not refrain from saying what he thought to be a historical truth. It was in his own words a "ghost unlaid." This compulsion is itself a sign of neurosis in the Freudian sense, and Ernest Jones in his three-volume biography of Freud, adulatory as it is, did not conceal the many neurotic traits of his subject and teacher.

For many years Freud could not overcome his inhibition about visiting Rome despite a strong yearning to see the Eternal City, and he was still in the throes of this inhibition when he wrote his book on dreams. But when he finally went there, subsequently returning to it again and again, one figure in its midst fascinated him and frightened him: "How often have I climbed the steep stairway of the ugly Corso Cavour to the lonely place where stands the deserted church and tried repeatedly to withstand the contemptuous-angry look of Moses; sometimes I slunk away from the twilight of the inner room as if I myself belonged to the mob who can not be faithful to any conviction, who can not wait and will not have confidence, and who cheers when given back the illusions of its idol."[3]

I do not intend to expand this discourse into an analytical exploration of Freud. On an earlier occasion I subjected to reexamination Freud's own dreams, dispersed among the dreams of his patients in *The Interpretation of Dreams*, and showed that at the time he wrote that book he had not overcome his hostility toward his father and was struggling with himself over whether or not to continue to adhere to his ancestral faith, a struggle from which he emerged victorious, only to resume it once more before the end of his life.[4] Jones, his biographer, disagreed with me but only at the cost of surrendering every analytical approach.[5] He had known Freud since 1908 and was acquainted with his emphatic proclamations of loyalty to his

[3] Freud, *Michelangelo.*

[4] "The Dreams Freud Dreamed," *Psychoanalytic Review*, XXVIII (1941), 487–511.

[5] Ernest Jones, *The Life and Work of Sigmund Freud*, II (1955), 17. Helen Walker Puner, in her biography of Freud (*Freud, His Life and His Mind* [1947], followed my interpretation, seeing in Freud's unresolved conflict with his father the cause of the subconsciously ambivalent stand toward his Jewishness. Erich Fromm in a recent book (*Sigmund Freud's Mission* [1959]) also formed his interpretation of Freud following this recognition of Freud's unresolved conflict.

race and ancestral faith, though Freud did not know the religious experience, the "oceanic feeling," as he called it. But Freud had written his book ten years earlier; and as the inner deliberations from dream to dream went on, he decided in 1898, first for himself, then for his children, to remain in the camp of those burdened with an ancient yoke and hampered in their social and scholastic advancement. And since when have conscious assertions and subconscious urges been regarded as identical by analysts?

Freud first published his work on Akhnaton and Moses in *Imago*, the same periodical in which, twenty-five years earlier, he had printed Abraham's paper on Akhnaton, quoted here on a previous page. But he did not refer to that paper and did not expend so much as a single sentence on Akhnaton's neurotic traits. He wrote about Akhnaton as though he had never read Abraham's paper or his own works about religion and monotheism, as if these subjects were above and beyond analysis. In analytical theory, however, God is nothing but the projection of the father image and its endowment with attributes of wisdom and power.

On the basis of his previous works, one might have expected Freud not only to acknowledge Abraham's insight into Akhnaton's Oedipus complex but also to elaborate on certain phenomena in Akhnaton's mental state. In *Totem and Taboo*, the first part of which was printed together with Abraham's paper in *Imago*, Freud discussed the custom, among many primitive peoples in various parts of the world, of not calling their dead by their names but giving them other names, and also of giving the survivors different names, for fear of conjuring up the spirit of the deceased. Akhnaton destroyed the name of his father and substituted for it on the monuments another name; he also changed his own name. Freud might also have considered the analytical meaning of the abrogation of a god and the symbolic meaning of the sun, father image in dreams,[6] and he might have applied to certain traits in Akhnaton his deep insight into the mechanism of paranoia. It is a disease in which the delusion of grandeur and the fear of persecution or of plotting are the most prominent characteristics. Freud studied a self-described case of paranoia written and published by a prominent jurist in the beginning of this century.[7] This person suffered from the delusion that he was destined to bring redemption to the human race, that solar energy was delivered to him in life-giving rays, as to nobody else—a concept very similar to the one we saw in Akhnaton; it is well known that "radiation" and "rays" play an important role in many case histories of schizophrenia.[8] The third delusional idea of the man studied by Freud was his impending metamorphosis and acquisition of a female body. The man turned his aggression on himself and effeminated all his being. It has been observed by several authors that a number of statues of Akhnaton are feminine in form and it is thought that he induced his sculptors to stress the feminine traits when portraying him.[9]

Were it possible for King Akhnaton to cross the time barrier and lie down on an analyst's couch, the analysis would at an early stage reveal autistic or narcissistic traits, a homosexual tendency, with sadism suppressed and feminine traits coming to the fore, and a strong unsuppressed Oedipus complex. The

[6] "Behold, I have dreamed a dream more; and, behold, the sun and the moon and the eleven stars made obeisance to me. And . . . his father rebuked him . . . Shall I and thy mother and thy brethren indeed come to bow down ourselves to thee to the earth?" (Genesis 37:9–10.)

[7] Freud, *Gesammelte Werke*, VIII (1943).

[8] "These rays are the prototype of the various kinds of radiation which have troubled paranoiacs through all the centuries." James Strachey, "Preliminary notes upon the problem of Akhenaten," *International Journal of Psycho-Analysis*, XX (1939), 33–42.

[9] "Akhenaten appears to have been born with an unusually large feminine component in his constitution." Ibid.

proper treatment of this historical Oedipus would not start by breaking down the Oedipus complex but by first demolishing the narcissistic component of his psychoneurosis.

When Freud approached Akhnaton he left behind all his experience and all his analytical tools. In analysis this is called repression. That there was something in the person of Akhnaton and in his acts which deeply affected Freud can be learned from an incident, described by Jones, which occurred in September 1913 in Munich. During a "discussion of Abraham's essay on Amenhotep, in which Abraham traced the Egyptian King's revolution to deep hostility against his father, [C. G.] Jung protested that too much was made of Amenhotep's erasing of his father's name and inscriptions wherever they occurred; any such death wishes were unimportant in comparison with the great deed of establishing monotheism." Freud, who was discussing with Jung Abraham's recently published paper, suddenly fainted and fell on the floor unconscious.[10] This episode should be recalled in considering Freud's repression of his entire psychoanalytical knowledge when he dealt with Akhnaton twenty-five years later.

Was Freud on the verge of some deep insight and, because of that, "blocked" as are analytical patients before an important truth reveals itself to them? I cannot dwell further here on Freud's intents and hidden motives, but I could not finish this study of the historical Oedipus and pass over in silence the man who elevated him to the greatest kingdom, the unconscious mind of all men.

[10] Jones, *The Life and Works of Sigmund Freud*, II, 147.

End

T H E legendary hero, or his historical prototype, marked by swollen lower extremities, spending his young years in exile away from his home in Thebes; his return, upon his father's death, to his homeland and kingdom, which for a short while had been ruled by the royal widow; his lack of reverence for the memory of his father, whose name he erased and whose memorial tablet he mutilated; his living in wedlock with his mother with whom he begot children; his popularity among his subjects and their affection for the king "who lives in truth" and was thought to be wise; the occurrence of some misfortune in the realm, which was blamed on the king's iniquity; the blindness of the king; his forced abdication after sixteen years of reign, imprisonment, and departure into exile; the role played in this palace revolution by the queen's brother; the agreement by which two young sons of the exiled king were to rule in turn; the refusal of the younger, still in his teens, to return the throne to the older when the latter's turn came; the support and guidance given in this matter to the prince on the throne by the same relative, the late queen's brother; the subsequent fraternal war, in which the exiled pretender was assisted by foreign armies; the death of both young brothers in the battle at besieged Thebes; the prohibition by the regent against the proper entombment of the fallen pretender, and the splendid

funeral rites accorded the fallen youthful king; the clandestine
entombment of the fallen rival by a pious sister and the desecration that followed; the imprisonment in a tomb-pit of the
princess for the act of mercy she committed; the taking over
of the crown and scepter by the old regent, the relative who,
during the entire period, had been scheming toward this end;
the role of the oracle to which human sacrifices were made, and
the equally prominent role of an old blind seer—all these elements are found both in the Greek drama about what happened
in the seven-gated Thebes in Boeotia and in the Egyptian history of what took place in the hundred-gated Thebes on the
Nile.

Single parallels between two sets of events can also be found
in situations of recorded history far apart in time. Thus, Henry
VIII broke with the Catholic Church as Akhnaton broke with
the cult of Amon, in order to contract a forbidden marriage,
and established his own church. Boris Godunov, a brother-in-law
of King Feodor, son of Ivan the Terrible, schemed for the
throne which he attained over the body of a slain boy-heir, not
unlike Creon, or Ay. George III, blind and profoundly despond-
ent, was a prisoner in his own palace, badly treated by his son,
who usurped power. But in the case before us there is not just
a single parallel; the entire tragedy of three generations is en-
acted in Thebes in Egypt and in the Theban trilogy of the
Greeks. To the preceding enumeration of parallel details we
could have added many more. We might have referred again
to Laius, the invert, and to Amenhotep III wearing a female
garment; or to Creon, whose children by his first wife, who died
in childbirth, were nursed by Jocasta, while Ay's second wife
nursed the child of his first wife who died young, also in childbirth; or to Oedipus being called "son of Helios [sun]" as was
Akhnaton.

There is no evidence of Akhnaton having killed his father;
however, "The hammering of the name was a veritable murder

. . . only the names of people condemned to death, or disgraced were hammered out."[1] And on the other hand an eminent scholar, Martin P. Nilsson, assumes that patricide might have been a later addition to the Oedipus legend.

The legend diverges from history by making the king who lived in incest with his mother ignorant of their blood relationship; and it was explained in this study how, by introducing this element of ignorance, events were made to take a fateful course, independent of the will of the participants, and the drama was Hellenized and heightened. In some of the instances we may also understand the origin of the names in the Greek legend: Laius means impudent effemination; Creon—a ruler; Oedipus—swollen legs; Polynices—belligerent.

Now we have an explanation for the absence of monuments or tombs of the heroes of the Oedipus legend in Boeotia and for the absence in that land of any cult connected with their memory in classical times. We understand also why the Greek legend has a cruel female monster, called the Sphinx, watching from a cliff overlooking Thebes. We know, too, why the original version of the legend had Oedipus marrying a second wife besides his mother and having children by both of them.

On the other hand, we understand why Akhnaton, upon ascending the throne, was unaware of the state of affairs of the kingdom, as the letters of the el-Amarna archives testify; why he erased the name of his father from the monuments but did not erase the names of Amenhotep I or his own containing the divine name Amon; and why he was so inimical to the cult of that god. We have likewise discovered the reason why the widowed queen kept a harem for the king; why her beauty, charm, and loveliness were extolled by her son, Akhnaton; why foreign potentates wrote to Akhnaton of "the mistress of thy house,"

[1] Lefébure, "La Vertu et la vie du nom en Egypte," quoted by A. Moret, "Revolution of Amenophis IV," p. 49. *Kings and Gods of Egypt* (1912).

meaning his mother Tiy; how Beketaten, a "child of the king's body," could have been born to Tiy more than six years after her husband's death; why Nefretete deserted Akhnaton and Tiy took her place; why Akhnaton, at first beloved by his subjects, was later proclaimed to have been a criminal and a sinner, and why he was dethroned and thereafter exiled; how Tiy ended her life, why a place of entombment entirely unfitting her position was prepared for her, and why her body was removed from there; and why Akhnaton was not buried in the royal tomb he had prepared for himself.

And, finally, we have learned why King Smenkhkare, son of Akhnaton, after a reign of a year or so was replaced on the throne by Tutankhamen, his younger brother; in what war Tutankhamen fought, as shown on a panel in his tomb; why both brothers died at such a young age; why Smenkhkare was entombed clandestinely and why some regalia, but not a crown or scepter, were placed in his grave; why Tutankhamen, a ruler in his teens, was afforded a burial of unprecedented magnificence; why his successor, Ay, had himself depicted as administering the rites in the young king's tomb; what made Ay so powerful that he could achieve the rank of a pharaoh; who was the prisoner immured in the pit-tomb in the Valley of the Kings; why and by whom the names of Amenhotep III, Akhnaton, and Smenkhkare were erased or changed on the monuments, and why Ay's tomb was demolished.

This was their life; this was the fate of their bodies in their tombs; this was also their afterlife in the Greek tragedies that carried through the centuries the story of their doom; this, finally, is their story as revealed by one modern author. He should not be condemned by the "winged maiden" for a mistaken answer, nor will he be given a kingdom for a true solution.

The Sphinx was an oracle, and therefore she was supposed to answer questions, not to ask them. Yet it is also true that oracular answers were often given in the form of a riddle that required interpretation, usually supplied by priests attending the oracle. In the legend of Oedipus, however, he has just come from the oracle of Delphi when he is stopped by the Sphinx and asked to solve a riddle about a creature with a changing number of legs. It has been observed that the answer Oedipus gave was on the level of a schoolboy and that the monster must have been feeble-minded to leap from the precipice upon hearing it. And why should a winged sphinx die in a jump? Innumerable authors have tried to solve the question of the Sphinx in different ways from that for which the hero was acclaimed. They range all the way from the "sexual curiosity of a child" (Freud) to an interesting thought put forward by W. B. Kristensen, that the Egyptian idea of the ever rejuvenating sun is the answer—the morning sun is represented hieroglyphically by a disk with the figure of a child (though not on all fours) and the evening sun by a disk with a figure of a man with a cane.

It does not seem to me that every question needs—or has—an answer. I have asked, instead, the Sphinx on the cliff in which direction to go. But were it my misfortune to stand before the Sphinx with the dire prospect of never entering Thebes, I should reply to her riddle: "It is Oedipus."

An oracle's questions and answers refer to the man who stands before it. Oedipus was exposed, a helpless infant with damaged feet, to crawl in the wasteland; he grew to be a man and a hero; his end was that of a blind wanderer in exile—"he shall make his way to a strange land, feeling the ground before him with his staff."[2] And I should add: "He was king in the Hundred-gated Thebes."

"Man," however, is a correct answer not to the riddle asked by the Sphinx but to the enigma of the Sphinx with its bestial

[2] *Oedipus Rex.*

body, human head, and wings, a creature animal, human, and divine: man is all this and the historical Oedipus was possessed by these three natures in the extreme.

> Wonders are many, and none is more wonderful than man. . . .
> And Earth, the unwearied, doth he wear. . . .
> And speech, and wind-swift thought, hath he taught himself;
> Only against Death shall he call for aid in vain.[3]

[3] Chorus, *Antigone*.